IMPROVING EDUCATIONAL
EVALUATION METHODS

Volume 11
SAGE RESEARCH PROGRESS SERIES IN EVALUATION

SAGE RESEARCH PROGRESS SERIES IN EVALUATION
Volume 11

Edited by
Carol B. Aslanian

IMPROVING EDUCATIONAL EVALUATION METHODS
Impact on Policy

Published in cooperation with the
EVALUATION RESEARCH SOCIETY

SAGE PUBLICATIONS   Beverly Hills   London

For information address:

SAGE Publications, Inc.
275 South Beverly Drive
Beverly Hills, California 90212

SAGE Publications Ltd
28 Banner Street
London EC1Y 8QE, England

Printed in the United States of America

Library of Congress Cataloging in Publication Data
Main entry under title:
Improving educational evaluation methods.

(Sage research progress series in evaluation ; v. 11)
Includes bibliographies.
Contents: Methodological basis of conflicting outcomes in policy research / Donna M. Mertens — Policy implications analysis, a method for improving policy research and evaluation / Doren L. Madey and A. Jackson Stenner — Randomized experiments at national, state, and local levels of government / Robert F. Boruch — [etc.]
   1. Educational surveys—United States—Addresses, essays, lectures. I. Aslanian, Carol B. II. Series.
LB2823.135   379.1'54   81-14615
AACR2

ISBN 0-8039-1729-5
ISBN 0-8039-1730-9 (Pbk.)

FIRST PRINTING

CONTENTS

Editor's Introduction
CAROL B. ASLANIAN   7

1 The Methodological Basis of Conflicting Outcomes
   in Policy Research
   DONNA M. MERTENS   11

2 Policy Implications Analysis: A Method for
   Improving Policy Research and Evaluation
   DOREN L. MADEY and A. JACKSON STENNER   23

3 Randomized Experiments at National, State, and
   Local Levels of Government: Recommendations
   from a Report to Congress
   ROBERT F. BORUCH   41

4 The Role of Experiments in Improving Education
   MARY M. KENNEDY   67

5 Evaluation of Curriculum Innovations: A Product
   Validation Approach
   JEROME JOHNSTON   79

6 The Comparability of Test Results Aggregated
   Across Test Batteries
   PAT A. THOMPSON and CARL D. NOVAK   101

7 Uses of Data to Improve Instruction in Local
   School Districts: Problems and Possibilities
   RICHARD C. WILLIAMS and ADRIANNE BANK   131

About the Authors   149

EDITOR'S INTRODUCTION

Policy formation in education suffers from the lack of conclusive evaluation data. Any evaluator who has ever shot at an invisible policy target, measured a program without measuring its competitors, judged new curriculum without knowing whether it was actually used, been unable to aggregate scores from different test batteries, or failed to persuade teachers to use test results to teach better will improve these skills by reading this book.

Audiences for evaluation data have traditionally felt shortchanged. Much too often, they do not get data to inform their decisions. Policy makers at the federal level are of particular importance in analyzing this problem. Their capacity to launch new programs, improve existing programs, and terminate ineffective programs is critical to an improved educational climate in this country. How can we as social scientists make them better able to do so?

It is one thing to see if a particular program works, it is another to find out if another program costs less and works, or costs the same but works better, or costs more but works much better. In our current state of shrinking educational budgets, we must apply methodologies which enable us to analyze relative costs and benefits so as to make greatest use of limited resources.

The educational research and development community and practitioners alike are well able to create new products for the schools. But, too often, the intended user—for one reason or another—fails to use these innovations to the degree necessary. Evaluations in such circumstances are invalid for they label the tested product ineffective when, in fact, it was never tried.

Testing and evaluation activities are becoming more important in our schools for a variety of reasons. Two problems which surround this phenomenon are addressed in this book. First, the proliferation of both national and local tests has enabled school districts to choose among many. While this opportunity fosters the matching of tests to local conditions, it also prevents us from pooling test results in order to judge school programs or explain student performance. The federal government is eager for data which can be aggregated for the purpose of setting national policy where appropriate. If data can be aggregated, the unpopular consequence of single, mandated tests could be avoided. Second, while most districts collect student test data, few take full advantage of the information they offer. District staff tend to use scores for summative rather than formative purposes. What can evaluators do to encourage the latter so that curriculum and instruction can learn from what students may or may not learn.

This book deals with ways in which evaluators can maximize the influence of policy research on policy decisions. Citing a history of both conflicting and inconclusive outcomes in the social sciences, the authors analyze methodological deficiencies and offer solutions.

In Chapter 1, Mertens describes the procedures and findings from a recent study on the effects of vocational education in order to illustrate some basic mismatches between what the research could illuminate and the information needs of policy makers. The study is useful in pointing out methodological constraints producing conflicting outcomes which, in turn, limit the use of the data. The author's basic question is: How can social scientists improve their evaluation procedures so as to better inform the decisions of policy makers? She identifies five major problems that must be solved.

Madey and Stenner, in Chapter 2, also emphasize the importance of addressing the data needs of policy makers. They offer a specific method, Policy Implications Analysis (PIA), which evaluators can use to solicit information needs of their audiences well before any evaluation design is shaped. PIA is a guide which helps evaluators conduct studies which place priorities of the client, policy makers in the cases presented, first. The six-step PIA process poses hypothetical findings to which potential users of the evaluation data must react. In so doing, PIA enables the evaluators to discern policy-relevant research questions that must be answered. The chapter supplies illustrations of how PIA has been applied in several federal programs. The authors conclude with a useful description of the disadvantages (such as time requirements and obstrusiveness) and advantages (such as consensus-building and explication of data needs) of the entire process.

Boruch, in Chapter 3, continues the discussion on how to affect public policy by calling for higher quality federally sponsored designs for assessing the effects of educational programs at the national, state, and local levels of government. His recommendations are based on recent findings from a study conducted for the Congress and the U.S. Department of Education. While referring to a variety of options for producing better designs, Boruch points to one recommendation in particular: that randomized experiments be authorized (that is, sanctioned, not required) at the federal level for the testing of new programs, variations of existing programs, and new program components. If our objective is to improve the performance of both schools and students, then higher-quality approaches which can estimate effects are needed, the author insists. The chapter includes other recommendations relevant to improving evaluation designs so that federal level decision-making will be better served.

One higher quality design option discussed by Boruch, randomized experiments, is underemployed. Why? Kennedy, in Chapter 4, suggests several answers for this phenomenon in local districts. She claims that low use of field experiments—a critical component of which is random assignment—is due less to inherent characteristics than to context problems. Examining the behavior of 25 local school districts, she identifies several obstacles, such as the preoccupation with immediate "how-to" questions at the district level rather than the resolution of competing options and the limited number of options actually available to districts. In short, field experiments are neither practical nor useful to the actual decisions that district leaders and staff must make. In describing this situation, the chapter surfaces conditions which would have to change to increase the likelihood that this method will be used at the district level.

New curricula must be proven effective before potential users will adopt them. Johnston, in Chapter 5, suggests that if they do not work, they may not have been used. Unfortunately, he claims, we are left much too often with the conclusion that curriculum innovations are ineffective when, in fact, they have not been implemented at sufficient levels to demonstrate their power. Using the television program *Freestyle,* Johnston introduces a new model for assessing effectiveness—product validation. The model calls for documenting acceptable levels of use before efficacy is studied. In so doing, product validation provides efficacy conclusions only if use is intensive enough to warrant them. Another advantage to the approach is its ability to produce efficacy data which can be used to convince potential users, such as teachers, of a product's merits. In short, product validation helps evaluators answer an important question about a new product: does it work when used?

Two major questions frequently surface during large-scale evaluations involving student performance: Do individual tests yield consistent results in different locations and at different times and are test results comparable across different test batteries? Thompson and Novak, in Chapter 6, shed light on these questions through their useful yet cautious responses based on testing experiences associated with the evaluation of the Elementary and Secondary Education Act Title I program. Their conclusions are important to making policy decisions about whether to mandate single tests or accept the results from multiple tests during the evaluation of major programs nationwide. The former would be necessary if test results from multiple tests could not be aggregated.

The book concludes with an analysis of an important problem today as testing and evaluation take on new significance in local school districts. The problem is that few districts actually use student test data to improve instructional practice. Williams and Bank, in Chapter 7, examine the characteristics of certain districts which do in fact make good use of the test data they collect. What promotes this practice? The authors examine local school districts and discuss the relative influence of factors such as administrative structure, parental pressure, and clarity of goals, to name only a few. Their impressions are valuable for those evaluators who wish to help local school districts use test data to improve instruction.

Donna M. Mertens
National Center For Research in Vocational Education

THE METHODOLOGICAL BASIS OF CONFLICTING OUTCOMES IN POLICY RESEARCH

INTRODUCTION

What type of information do policy makers find useful in formulating human resource policy? Florio et al. (1979: 69) addressed this question through a study of congressional staff members. They found that the credibility of social science research has been questioned by policy makers, as is exemplified by the comments of the congressional staff members. For example, one staff member remarked, "All social science suffers from the perception that it is unreliable and not policy-relevant." Other congressional staffers commented that "research rarely provides definitive conclusions," or "for every finding, others negate it," or "educational research can rarely be replicated and there are few standards that can be applied to assess the research products." Another common complaint was that reports and findings often revealed conflicting outcomes and interpretations.

Florio et al. suggested means that researchers could use to better meet the needs of the policy maker. They suggested that the most needed areas of information were related to program and policy ef-

AUTHOR'S NOTE: The research reported herein was supported in part by Contract Number OEC-300-78-0032 from the Department of Education, Office of Vocational and Adult Education. The views expressed are those of the author.

fects, and, more specifically, student achievement data. Among the methods for improving the usefulness of educational studies, Florio et al. (1979: 69) recommend preparation of reports that "do not have results which are overly cautious."

The purpose of this chapter is to examine the source of conflicts that arise between social science research and the expressed desires of policy makers, in the context of a specific policy study. Because the policy study under consideration was a review and synthesis of literature concerning the effects of an educational program, two levels of methodological considerations emerged. First, the problems of conducting a review and synthesis study are explored in terms of the methodology and the interpretation of results. Second, methodological considerations for the conduct of primary research and evaluation studies are discussed. Finally, recommendations for improving the responsiveness of the social scientist to policy makers are provided.

THE POLICY STUDY

High youth unemployment combined with severe national economic problems have led the Congress to focus on vocational education and other youth employment initiatives. The effects, or outcomes, from participation in vocational education are probably the most debated policy questions relevant to vocational education. Those who must decide how public funds are to be used need more and better information to help them choose among competing alternatives. Vocational education, because of its apparent potential to deal with many of the nation's serious problems, is especially being called upon to demonstrate the effects it can produce.

Therefore, the National Center for Research in Vocational Education undertook a study of the effects of vocational education for the purpose of providing information to policy makers (Mertens et al., 1980). The study attempted to assemble and summarize all studies that could be obtained on the effects of participating in vocational education that were reported from 1968 through 1979. An extensive search of published sources and solicitation of unpublished reports yielded a total of 1489 unduplicated titles. After irrelevant studies were eliminated, a total of 232 reports were identified which contained data on the effects of public vocational education at the secondary or postsecondary level. These were classified into more rigorous, less rigorous, national, and review and synthesis studies.

Two problems that face the researcher who is conducting a review and synthesis study are which studies to include and what criteria to use for inclusion. Researchers do not agree on the solution to these problems. Glass and Smith (1976) recommend including all studies that present sufficient information for computing effect sizes and looking for differences in study characteristics. They contend that it is dysfunctional to institute rigorous inclusion standards. Eysenck (1978), on the other hand, criticizes lenient standards as "abandonment of scholarship." Referring to the efficiency of psychotherapy, he stated that no study has been conducted with sufficient methodological rigor to provide useful information as to its efficacy. Pillemer and Light (1980) take the middle of the road and suggest that all studies included in a synthesis should adhere to certain basic standards for research reporting. They also state (1980: 192), "While it seems sensible to exclude studies that fail to meet basic acceptability standards, it is also important to realize that different types of studies may produce different outcomes simply because they are designed to elicit different information."

In order to discriminate between "more" and "less" rigorous studies, criteria were established for screening the studies. A study was categorized as "less" rigorous if it met one or more of the following criteria:

(1) Studies based on very small samples (25 subjects or less).
(2) Studies that did not describe their methodology in adequate detail.
(3) Studies with less than a 40 percent response rate, unless the researcher reported information about nonrespondents.
(4) Studies that lacked some standard of comparison.

If a study had a large enough sample (that is, over 25), included an adequate description of its methodology, and had a response rate of 40 percent or more (or the researcher reported on nonrespondents), and included some standard of comparison, then it was termed "more" rigorous. As was alluded to earlier, scholars can debate the criteria for inclusion ad infinitum. The stated criteria were judged to be relevant for this review.

Studies based on national data bases were not screened on the basis of methodological rigor. The primary national data bases included in the review were Project Talent, National Longitudinal Surveys (of Labor Market Experience; NLS), the Longitudinal Study of Educational Effects (Class of 1972), and the American College Testing Career Assessment Program (ACT). (Grasso and Shea [1979] provide an overview of these four studies.)

Even with this screening process, derivation of firm conclusions was difficult. Many of the complaints of respondents in the Florio et al. (1979) study could be applied to this data set. A brief summary of the study's findings are presented below. The results of the study are used to illustrate the difficulty of interpreting the data and drawing unequivocal conclusions.

Study Conclusions and Limitations

Although many questions remain unanswered, sufficient evidence exists to indicate that (at least at the postsecondary level) participation in vocational education is associated with high levels of employment, or conversely, less unemployment. Most vocational students (some figure greater than 50 percent at the secondary and even higher at the postsecondary level) are obtaining jobs in the occupational areas in which they were trained. This suggests that these former students are being hired for jobs that require specialized training. In addition, the preponderance of evidence suggests that employers are satisfied with vocational graduates and that these graduates are satisfied with their jobs.

The evidence on other variables is not so encouraging. Some studies found vocational students earned more initially, but the difference disappeared after approximately five years. Other studies found no such advantage. Obviously, stronger evidence of income effects is needed to claim that vocational education can be an effective means of reducing poverty. On the other hand, the lack of significant income differences suggests that participation in vocational education does not automatically lead to "less financially rewarding" jobs.

Too little evidence is available to comment on the effects of vocational education for individuals with special needs or its effects in overcoming sex stereotyping.

With regard to educational effects, vocational graduates report being satisfied with training. Insufficient information is available to draw conclusions concerning the effects on basic skill and specific occupational skill acquisition. About one-third of vocational graduates continue their education beyond the secondary level. While this is lower than the percentage of nonvocational graduates, it does suggest that the doors to higher education are not closed to vocational graduates. The question concerning whether vocational education prevents students from dropping out of school cannot be answered from the available evidence.

These, then, are the major findings of this review. How one interprets them will depend, of course, upon the evaluative standards applied. Assuming the actual rate of placement in related occupations is somewhere between 50 and 75 percent, is this acceptable or not? Recognizing that many students, at both the secondary and post-secondary levels, use vocational courses for purposes of occupational exploration, a 100 percent rate is neither likely nor desirable. Our educational system attempts to facilitate individual choices at all levels. A 100 percent rate would indicate to many observers that vocational programs are too effective in directing students to a limited range of potential occupations.

On the other hand, very low rates of related placement would also be undesirable. They would indicate that most of the investment made to reach occupational skills was not yielding a return through the use of these skills in the labor force. Whatever standard is set will involve a tradeoff between consideration of enhancing individual choice and options and realizing the best possible return on investment in human capital.

With regard to the uncertainty regarding income advantages, Gustman and Steinmeier (1979: vi) recently presented a thoeoretical analysis that concludes: "we have seen that a vocational training program may produce maximum benefits to the workers at precisely that point where earnings differentials are narrowed to zero." This one analysis is unlikely to change the widely held expectation that vocational programs should yield labor market advantages. Nevertheless, this essay suggests that the fact that many studies have not detected consistent earnings and employment advantages for vocationally trained workers may be due to the way the labor market operates rather than deficiencies in vocational programs or in the studies that have examined them.

The evidence does indicate that vocational education is providing meaningful, employment-related education for many young people who do not plan to continue their education, and it is helping to meet the skill needs of employers. On the two criteria specified for evaluation in the Education Amendments of 1976—job-related placement and employer satisfaction—vocational educational measures up rather well, if related placement in the 50 to 75 percent range is considered acceptable. The evidence on the broader social goals is either inconclusive or nonexistent at this time.

The inconclusiveness of the findings from the review and synthesis arise in part from the methodologies used in the studies that were included. General methodological considerations for primary research and evaluation studies are discussed below.

GENERAL METHODOLOGICAL CONSIDERATIONS

A number of general methodological considerations in conducting research on the effects of vocational education underlie the tentativeness of the study's conclusions. The methodological considerations, for the most part, are applicable to social science research in general.

Self-Selection Bias

Traditional research methodology calls for random assignment of subjects to experimental treatments in order to determine the effect of each treatment in an independent manner. Obviously, school systems are not free to randomly assign students to a vocational, general, or academic curriculum. As a result, systematic differences in the types of persons enrolled in each program may account for more of the variance in effects than the programs themselves.

Grasso and Shea (1979) present empirical differences between students in vocational education and other curricula in terms of selected demographic characteristics (such as SES, race, ability, and sex). Stromsdorfer (1972) suggests that members of these groups may also vary on other characteristics such as value of earnings, job status, additional college education and other factors associated with the multiple outcomes of education. This self-selection bias is a threat to validity. It is recognized that even sophisticated statistical techniques cannot isolate progam effects in a self-selected sample. However, careful description of sample characteristics can alert the researcher to systematic differences that need to be taken into account. Few of the studies included in the review and synthesis study provided sufficient demographic information about the participants.

Definition of the Program

Vocational education programs can vary in quality, content, intensity, and duration. As Pillemer and Light (1980) point out, similarly labeled treatments or programs may differ in important ways. The question arises, "Do programs with the same labels offer the same services?" Grasso and Shea (1979) noted that none of the national surveys seem to include information on the process by which students choose or are tracked into a vocational program or change curricula enrollment. Grasso (1979) suggested that the extent to which a student changes from one curriculum to another will affect the validity of an effectiveness measure. In very few instances is there an attempt to define vocational education in the studies included in the review and synthesis study.

Identification of Students

Three methods have typically been used to determine a student's classification into a general, academic, or vocational program: self-report, administrator's designation, and use of student transcripts. Grasso and Shea (1979) noted that the National Longitudinal Study of the High School Class of 1972 obtained information from all three sources. An examination of the results reveals substantial disagreement among the three methods. They present the conclusion that neither the administrators' nor the students' reports adequately describe the pattern of courses. The most frequent methods used in the studies included in the review and synthesis study were self-identification and administrator identification. Only rarely were transcripts used to identify the students' curriculum.

Reliability and Validity of Dependent Measures

Many of the national, regional, state, and local studies did not report reliability or validity data for their measurement instrument. However, Conger et al.'s (1976) study of the reliability of a subsample of items in the Class of 1972 survey does provide some insight into this matter. They found that contemporaneous, objective, factually oriented items are more reliable than subjective, temporally remote, or ambiguous items. They also found that reports of income are generally of low reliability and validity. Interview-collected data tended to be more reliable than mail-in data. They also reported a number of interactions for selected demographic subgroups, that is, by ethnicity, SES, ability, and sex.

One exceptional study at the state level was reported by Pucel and Luftig (1975). They examined the reliability of the student vocational follow-up system developed at the University of Minnesota. They found very high reliabilities (82 to 100 percent) for items pertaining to an individual's work history, with the exception of salary information and number of months employed. Moderately high reliabilities (79 to 91 percent) were reported for items pertaining to the graduates' judgments of the facilities, equipment, instruction, and whether or not they would choose the same program again. Lower reliabilities (57 to 78 percent) were reported for items pertaining to training curriculum and community services (with the exception of placement assistance). Pucel and Luftwig (1975: 19) concluded that "the data gathered from the student follow-up questionnaire are sufficiently reliable to be used as one source of information in decision making concerning vocational programs."

Contextual Factors

The vocational education legislation places emphasis on students obtaining occupations related to their training. However, employment is affected by other factors, such as the state of the economy and the labor market. Earnings is another variable that is commonly used to measure the effectiveness of vocational education. Yet, evidence does suggest that this variable is influenced to a considerable degree by unionization (Freedman, 1976).

IMPLICATIONS FOR FUTURE RESEARCH

Obviously, not all of these methodological considerations are amenable to manipulation by the researcher. Nevertheless, two types of implications for future research emerge. First, a general discussion relating to the research methodology and reporting is presented. This is followed by a discussion of the need to formulate research questions which will provide information that is relevant for policy-making.

Research Methodology and Reporting

The problem of locating and acquiring research concerning the effects of vocational education has important implications for researchers. The methods for locating research for this review included the major computerized data bases, libraries, personal contacts with authors and state departments, as well as the National Advisory Council for Vocational Education. Despite the thoroughness of the search, it is recognized that all possible research was not located. Researchers have an obligation to the educational community to report their findings in such a manner that they are accessible to others.

In terms of reporting research, more emphasis should be given to describing the educational program in order for researchers to know what the "treatment" actually is. Researchers should also report the methodology used more completely and clearly, including sample size and response rates. More attention should also be given to reporting contextual factors which influence the effects of educational programs (such as unionization in specific occupations and economic conditions in communities).

Concerning the methodology used in the studies, dependent variables should be chosen intelligently in order for them to represent legitimate outcomes for vocational education. The definition of dependent variables also presents a problem, especially for such variables as employment, unemployment, and earnings. Standardization of definitions would ensure that results are comparable across studies. In addition, definition of the independent variable of "curriculum" raises a problem. Methods for classifying subjects as vocational, academic, or general need attention. Use of actual transcripts with decision rules can insure a more accurate classification.

Finally, the reliability and validity of instruments should be established and reported. Because earnings is an important indicator, research should be undertaken to improve the reliability of this measure. If sound conclusions are to be drawn concerning the effects of vocational education, sound research must be more pervasively conducted, reported and disseminated.

Research Questions

If social scientists are to be responsive to the needs of policy makers, they must provide appropriate information based on the review of the vocational education literature. The following areas are in need of additional research.

Equity is an overriding issue that is not adequately addressed by the existing body of research. Comparisons of male and female earnings underscore the importance of the equity issue. The effects of vocational education on special needs groups such as the handicapped and disadvantaged emerged as an area in need of further research. In addition, the area of equity for both sexes and all races is an important issue in need of more research.

The areas of attendance and dropout need additional research to answer the question, "Can vocational education retain students in school who might otherwise have dropped out?" Also, what can be done to help dropouts after they have left school? The high rate of dropouts for minorities and those enrolled in nontraditional programs is another area of concern. Another question in need of research is, "What role can counseling play in reducing dropout rates?"

The attainment of basic skills is an area in need of further research from two perspectives. First, the current level of attainment should be more carefully studied. Second, the proper balance in the curriculum between basic skill and occupational skill attainment should be explored. In addition, better measurement and reporting of occupational skill attainment is needed. This raises the question of how specific training should be, particularly at the secondary level. The research question of interest is: "Should emphasis be given to training students in specific occupational skills or in more general employability skills?"

Three additional areas of research are related to the continuing education variable. First, examination of and control for continuing education activities outside the traditional school system should be included in future research. The second question concerns the degree of preparedness for postsecondary education that is experienced by secondary vocational graduates. Third, less research was found for postsecondary than secondary effects, especially at the national level, indicating that more attention to this area is needed.

Measures of employer satisfaction are confounded because of a lack of equivalency in the types of jobs held by vocational and nonvocational graduates. Future research of employer satisfaction should explore ways to account for this variation.

A much small body of data was located for inclusion in this review for ancillary effects than for education and employment. If the areas of aspirations, attitudes and values, feelings of success, and citizenship are judged to be important effects of vocational education, then these areas are in need of further research.

CONCLUSION

Simple answers to policy questions will never exist, much to the chagrin of both policy makers and researchers. Many authors have made recommendations to researchers on how to improve their responsiveness to policy makers' needs (Coleman, 1972; Florio et al., 1979; Pincus, 1980). While following such recommendations has the potential to yield better information for policy makers, it will not make the "real world" complexities go away. Harsh reality will forever limit the research methodologies and will result in conflicting findings. Perhaps this tension between researcher and policy maker will serve as a creative impetus to provide better answers to the social policy questions of this generation.

REFERENCES

COLEMAN, J. S. (1972) Policy Research in the Social Sciences. Morristown, NJ: General Learning Press.

CONGER, A. J., J. C. CONGER, and J. A. RICCOBONO (1976) Reliability and Validity of National Longitudinal Study Measures: An Empirical Reliability Analysis of Selected Data and Review of the Literature on the Validity and Reliability of Survey Research Questions. Research Triangle Park, NC: Research Triangle Institute.

EYSENCK, H. J. (1978) "An exercise in mega-silliness." American Psychologist 33: 517.

FLORIO, D. H., M. M. BERHMANN, and D. L. GOLTZ (1979) "What do policy makers think of educational research and evaluation? Or do they?" Educational Evaluation and Policy Analysis 1, 6: 61-87.

FREEDMAN, M. (1976) Labor Markets: Segments and Shelters. Montclair, NJ: Allenheld, Osmun.

GLASS, G. V. and M. L. SMITH (1976) "Meta-analysis of psychotherapy outcome studies." Presented at the annual meeting of the Society for Psychotherapy Research, San Diego, June.

GRASSO, J. T. (1979) Impact Evaluation: The State of the Art. Columbus, OH: The National Center for Research in Vocational Education.

——— and J. R. SHEA (1979) Effects of Vocational Education Programs: Research Findings and Issues. The Planning Papers for the Vocational Education Study. Washington, DC: Government Printing Office.

GUSTMAN, A. L. and T. L. STEINMEIER (1979) Labor Market Effects and Evaluations of Vocational Training Programs in the Public High Schools—Toward a Framework for Analysis. Report to the Assistant Secretary for Planning and Evaluation, USDHEW, December.

MERTENS, D. M., D. McELWAIN, G. GARCIA and M. WHITMORE (1980) The Effects of Participating in Vocational Education. Columbus: The National Center for Research in Vocational and Technical Education, Ohio State University. (RD202).

PILLEMER, D. P. and R. J. LIGHT (1980) "Synthesizing outcomes: how to use research evidence from many studies." Harvard Educational Review 50, 2: 176-195.

PINCUS, J. [ed.] (1980) Educational Evaluation in the Public Policy Setting. Santa Monica, CA: The Rand Corporation.

PUCEL, D. J. and J. T. LUFTWIG (1975) The Reliability of the Minnesota Vocational Follow-Up Student Questionnaire. Minneapolis: University of Minnesota.

STROMSDORFER, E. W. (1972) Review and Synthesis of Cost-Effectiveness Studies of Vocational and Technical Education. Columbus: The Center for Vocational and Technical Education, Ohio State University, August (ED 066 554).

2

Doren L. Madey
A. Jackson Stenner
NTS Research Corporation

POLICY IMPLICATIONS ANALYSIS:
A Method for Improving Policy
Research and Evaluation

INTRODUCTION

Enhancing the utility of evaluations is a shared goal of policy makers and evaluators alike (Filstead, 1980; Gideonse, 1980; Pincus, 1980; Bailey, 1979; Bissell, 1979; Patton, 1978; Weiss, 1977). To alter the destiny of the typical evaluation report from gathering dust on a bookshelf to guiding administrative action requires new approaches and methodologies. Although approaches for increasing use of evaluation results for decision-making have been documented (Madey, 1980; Smith, 1980; Bissell, 1979; Hayman et al., 1979; Patton, 1978), few formal methods exist. The need for such methods has been expressed recently from several perspectives (Berryman and Glennan, 1980; Hill, 1980; Weiler and Stearns, 1980). Filstead (1980), for example, argues that policy makers should insist that procedures

AUTHORS' NOTE: This chapter was first presented as a paper at the Fourth Annual Meeting of the Evaluation Research Society, Washington, D.C., November 19-21, 1980. The NTS evaluation of the State Capacity Building Program is supported with federal funds from the National Institute of Education, Department of Education; however, the contents of this chapter do not necessarily reflect the views or policies of the National Institute of Education or the Department of Education. Reprints may be obtained by writing the authors at the following address: NTS Research Corporation, 2634 Chapel Hill Boulevard, Durham, N.C. 27707.

be employed to gather policy-relevant data from interested or involved parties. *Policy Implications Analysis* (PIA) (Stenner and Madey, 1976) is one such method designed to maximize the likelihood that an evaluation report will have an impact on decision-making. PIA was designed to help people who were planning and conducting evaluations to tailor their information so that it had optimal potential for being used and acted upon. This chapter describes the development and application of Policy Implications Analysis.

The chapter is organized in four parts. First, the need for formal methods to enable decision makers to specify more explicitly their information requirements is briefly discussed. Second, one such method designed to meet this need, PIA, is described in enough detail to permit other investigators to apply the approach to their own studies. In the third section, a recently completed evaluation is used to illustrate the method's application. Finally, associated advantages and disadvantages of the method are presented.

NEED

The importance of designing evaluations so as to meet policymakers' information requirements is a current and recurring theme. Pincus (1980: 3-4) describes the typical situation:

> Most policymakers want their programs to succeed; but most "scientific" evaluations address effects and indicate that student outcomes as measured by test scores, dropout rates, and other such measures appear to be little affected by new government agency programs. Such reports of "no significant effect" are generally unaccompanied by useful recommendations for program improvement or policy change. Meanwhile, policymakers seek to know not only about effects, but also about what is going on in the program: how the resources are being used, whether implementation corresponds to program intent, and who is benefiting from program resource use. In effect, what can result is a "dialog of the deaf," in which neither party understands the other's premises.

Hill (1980) argues that evaluation planning must begin with a careful assessment of policy makers' information needs beginning, in the case of a federally mandated study, with the Congress. Likewise, Berryman and Glennan (1980) argue that appropriate evaluation methods for a federal program cannot be defined without reference to the policy-making process. Berryman and Glennan state that the policy-making process is political in that it involves real value conflicts; because no one party can impose a solution to the conflicts, policy-making becomes a mechanism for resolving differences or a process of compromise. To be most useful, then, evaluations should address different outcomes and processes. Berryman and Glennan add that realities often dictate that the interests of the party funding the evaluation are primary. To establish agreement about the evaluation's goals and appropriate research designs, Weiler and Stearns (1980) argue for increased collaboration among evaluators and government agencies. The goal of evaluators' work must be to provide policy makers with information which will help their deliberations.

PIA was designed to improve communication between the evaluators and policy makers by providing an active forum through which information users could express their information needs. PIA is based on the assumption that a more responsive and useful evaluation will result by understanding both the policy context within which the evaluation is commissioned and also the questions being posed by actors within that context. PIA enables the evaluation team to understand what the policy decisions are likely to be and to identify the types of information that will be needed to make these decisions.

DESCRIPTION

PIA is a six-step process designed to explicate the information requirements of key information users at a variety of levels (such as federal, state, and local). Active participation by both evaluators and policy makers is necessary throughout the process. The PIA method proceeds as follows:

Step 1. Statements of hypothetical, but theoretically possible, findings which could result from the evaluation are generated. The findings range from being very straightforward and in line with previous studies to being relatively unexpected (in relation to previous theory and practice). Formal or informal involvement of key information users may be sought during this first step.

Step 2. Using the generated hypothetical findings, a written exercise is prepared for later use with a carefully selected panel of respondents. The exercise is comprised of four major sections:
  • an introduction to the exercise which briefly describes the PIA method and the program under scrutiny;

- hypothetical findings or "scenarios" which might appear in an executive summary of a future evaluation report with guidelines for responding to the hypothetical findings;
- an opportunity for respondents to generate findings which might result in a decision to drastically revamp or eliminate the program; and
- an evaluation of the overall exercise.

Step 3.   A carefully selected panel of respondents, representing a cross-section of policy makers and other information users at a variety of levels (such as federal, state, and local) is identified. Both proponents and opponents of the program are included in the respondent group.

Step 4.   Each member of the respondent panel is asked to complete the exercise. Respondents read the hypothetical statements and respond to each finding in terms of the following:
- how likely they feel it is that the finding will actually result from the study;
- what policy actions they consider feasible should the finding be sustained; and
- what further information would be needed to modify policy or take action based on the finding (that is, what additional questions would be posed?).

Step 5.   The responses of the individuals are analyzed and synthesized to:
- clarify the expectations of relevant stakeholder groups regarding the evaluation, and
- delineate the context within which the evaluation is embedded.

Step 6.   The analyzed responses are used to develop a set of policy-relevant questions or hypotheses which then guide the creation of a conceptual framework for the evaluation.

The PIA method builds upon two futures techniques: the Delphi Method and Scenario Writing. The Delphi Method is a procedure for eliciting and refining ideas and gaining consensus from a panel of experts about possible future states or conditions. Typically, the procedure involves several "probes" of a panel utilizing a questionnaire, and then aggregating and feeding back the findings until group consensus is achieved. It should be noted that one of the key purposes of Delphi is *not* a purpose of PIA. Iterative probes are not used to reach a unified consensus from the panel of respondents; rather, the purpose is to uncover and explicate diverse expectations and information needs emanating from different perspectives on future policy-making and decision-making, and then to use this information to design an evaluation that meets, to the extent possible, all information users' needs. As is the case with the Delphi procedure, several sequential PIA exercises may be utilized to increase the quantity and quality of design-relevant information.

Scenario Writing, a technique perfected by Herman Kahn and popularized by the book *The Year 2000* (Kahn and Weiner, 1967) involves the generation of carefully calculated stories about the future. Scenarios have two important advantages that are relevant to the hypothetical findings generated in the PIA exercise: first, they call attention to the larger range of possibilities that must be considered, and second, they illustrate forcefully certain principles or questions which would be ignored if one insisted on taking examples only from the present world. In the PIA exercise, the interest is on forecasting "findings" and generating policy "scenarios" for more than just a given time frame—for example, one year—in the future. In effect, the intent is to look ahead to the long-range unfolding of an evaluation process. Thus, in the PIA exercise, one must be especially alert not to be overly constrained by the routinely "plausible" and "conventional" in making hypothetical projections.

APPLICATION

PIA has been used successfully by NTS Research Corporation in several longitudial evaluations of federal programs (see Madey et al., 1980; McNeil et al., 1980). An illustration of the method's application in the recently completed evaluation of the State Capacity Building Program for the National Institute of Education (NIE), Department of Education, is presented in this section. Prior to illustrating how PIA has been used in such an evaluation, it is helpful to describe the specific program and evaluation to be used in the example. Therefore, a brief overview of the State Capacity Building Program and its evaluation is first presented.[1]

The State Capacity Building Program and Its Evaluation

Through the NIE-sponsored State Capacity Building Program (established in 1975 and still operating), state education agencies (SEAs) are awarded one-year, renewable grants of about $100,000 each to support the development and eventual institutionalization of statewide dissemination systems to make current educational knowledge and practices accessible to administrators and practitioners. According to the NIE program announcements, such systems are to be comprised of three generic components: (1) an information resource base which contains the knowledge or knowledge-based products clients need, (2) linkages to connect the resources with the people who could benefit from them, and (3) a leadership/management component to coordinate the various activities needed so local educators could use the system for school improvement. From these generic components, states are expected to develop specific systems, customized to their own contexts, which extend or adapt existing structures for enhancing dissemination services; and as a collaborative effort between NIE and the states, time lines are established by mutual agreement.

Under the sponsorship of the Research and Educational Practice unit of NIE's Program on Dissemination and Improvement of Practice, NTS Research Corporation conducted a study for the first four years (1975-1979) of operation of the State Capacity Building Program. The purpose of this study was not to evaluate the success of specific capacity building projects, but rather to identify factors which facilitate or impede SEA efforts to build and institutionalize statewide dissemination systems. The NTS study was intended to develop an understanding of how federal and state policies might permit capacity building for this program and for future capacity-building programs. The NTS study was also intended to provide both federal and state decision makers with useful information for improving current and future programs.

An Illustration

Exactly how the PIA method was used in the evaluation of the State Capacity Building Program is explained in this section on a step-by-step basis. Where appropriate, samples from the respondents' completed exercises are included. The intent is to provide sufficient information for other evaluation designers and implementers interested in customizing the method for use in other program evaluations.

When NTS Research Corporation was awarded the contract to evaluate NIE's State Capacity Building Grants Program, the study's major audiences' information needs were not clearly specified. NTS researchers designed PIA to help clarify the various audiences' information needs so that the evaluation results would have the optional potential for being used.[2]

To begin, hypothetical findings were generated for each of the three generic component areas included in the program evaluation. A total of 29 finding statements were generated, 13 for information resources, 8 for linkages, and 8 for leadership/management. The NTS project team was assisted by several state project directors. In the initial exercise, federal program personnel were not involved in generating the hypothetical finding statements; however, subsequent exercises included federal personnel, as well.

Using the generated hypothetical findings, a written exercise was prepared following the outline presented in Figure 2.1. (The generic outline was used to design additional PIA exercises as well.)

To respond to the exercise, a carefully selected panel, representing a cross-section of policy makers and other information users at a variety of levels, was identified. Respondents included federal program managers, federal project monitors, state project directors, and recognized experts in the field.

Each member of the respondent panel was asked to complete the exercise. Respondents read the hypothetical findings and responded to the included guidelines and probes. All invited panel members completed the exercise. Sample responses to three hypothetical finding statements are presented in the appendix. All such responses were analyzed to clarify the expectations of relevant stakeholder groups and to delineate the context within which the evaluation was embedded.

In this particular study, PIA revealed that the federal program staff had a greater interest in understanding program design and management factors than had been originally thought. PIA also revealed that although evaluation information would be useful at the state level, the primary clients were personnel at the federal level. Many state projects would be completed before the final evaluation report was published and disseminated.

Finally, the analyzed responses were used to develop a refined set of policy-relevant questions. Prior to administering PIA, two initial design questions had been framed:

- Is capacity being built as a result of this program?
- Is the program having an effect? If so, what is the nature of the effect?

Actual findings were summarized under three policy research questions:

- Is dissemination capacity being built?
- What are the factors affecting the building of capacity? What factors help or hinder achievement of program objectives?
- What program management and program design factors affect the building of capacity?

Thus, the PIA exercise provided information which enabled the NTS evaluators to refine the major study questions and final study design. If requests for the final report are indicative of the study's value, then the evaluation has been useful to federal policy makers, state project directors, and other policy researchers and evaluators alike. Although not by any means the sole contributing factor, PIA did, in the evaluators' views, make a difference in the study's utility.

ASSOCIATED DISADVANTAGES AND ADVANTAGES

Enumerating the pros and cons of any method is a useful exercise. The potential disadvantages and advantages associated with PIA are summarized in this section.

Potential Disadvantages

Perhaps no technique is without potential disadvantages, and PIA is no exception. Some of the difficulties surround the implementation of the technique and are presumably correctible through refinements in the process. Other problems stem from the inherently obtrusive character of the technique itself.

The technique takes time, a commodity that is often rare in the initial stages of an evaluation. If a single polling of respondents is all that is desired, then the entire process of scenario design, administration, and analysis can be accomplished in six weeks. If, however, it is important to employ feedback and arrange sharing of respondents' comments, then several iterations may be desirable, each requiring, at a minimum, one month.

Selection of the panel can be problematic. Diversity of position and persuasion is essential but either too much diversity or diversity at the expense of representativeness can be self-defeating. The ideal is to adequately represent the major constituencies that will finally use the evaluation information. In some evaluations, there may be only one user group whereas in others, such as the evaluations of Head Start and the State Capacity Building Program, the range might run from local program staff to Congress. It should be apparent that an inappropriate panel selection will hamper the generalizability and, thus, utility of panel responses.

Related to the issue of panel selection is the fact that policy contexts are dynamic and the important actors and/or information users may change with time. A partial solution to this problem is an annual polling of users accompanied by a reassessment of each user's continuing relevance. Of course, this solution is less effective in highly dynamic contexts in which the significant actors, or political climate, frequently change.

Lastly, Policy Implications Analysis is obtrusive and may reawaken dormant policy issues which are best left alone. The technique may promote frustration by encouraging participants to explore policy actions and alternatives for which adequate information does not exist (at the time) to reach an informed decision. Depending upon the policy context, the energy generated as a by-product of the technique may be viewed as desirable or undesirable.

Selected Advantages

Even with such disadvantages, PIA represents a methodological advancement for policy research and evaluation. Inherent in the technique are substantial advantages:

- Policy makers' and other information users' expectations and preconceptions regarding the evaluation and its findings are made explicit.
- Policy alternatives are delineated, and supporting information requirements for each alternative are identified (that is, evaluation questions are formulated).
- The connections between evaluation information and alternative policy actions are given additional clarity.
- Areas of consensus and disagreement among information users are identified. For example, information needs of program staff and higher-level policy makers are not always congruent; thus, perceptions of the purpose and benefit of the evaluation may differ.

- Possible unintended outcomes are unmasked by involving information users who are not totally supportive of the program. Such outcomes generally go unaddressed when intentions and program design comprise the sole foundation upon which the evaluation is built.
- Boundaries for the evaluation, and information priorities within these boundaries, are made explicit.
- Results of the PIA exercise often result in deflating unrealistic expectations regarding what can be learned from an evaluation.
- A large number of respondents may be involved in the process without restrictions imposed by geography. The process is relatively low in cost, compared to the benefits derived from using such a tool.
- If desired, the entire process can be accomplished with anonymity for the participants, thus avoiding unnecessary ideological battles and policy confrontations which might better await the arrival of objective evaluation information.

Most importantly, though, PIA has already been used successfully to enhance the utility of evaluation results for decision makers. This formal method fills a critical need, and the NTS Research Corporation's experiences with PIA suggest that it may be useful to others as well. The response to the statement "evaluations aren't useful" should no longer be tacit agreement. PIA can be used to help evaluators design and implement studies which meet policy makers' needs.

Leadership/Mangement

A. Hypothetical Finding

In 11 of the 24 states, the State Capacity Building Grant accounts for less than 10 percent of the total SEA expenditures for dissemination. In these states the impact of no State Capacity Building Grant would be largely inconsequential in terms of either the large number of services available in the state or the quality of the delivery mechanisms. These same states have key leaders funded outside the grant who are well entrenched in the power structure and who appear to be developing statewide capacity largely independent of the State Capacity Building Grant.

B. Guidelines (circle your response)

1. To what degree is this finding within the purview of the NTS evaluation?

Definitely within   Definitely without

1   (2)   3   4   5   6   7   8   9   10

2. How much knowledge do you have of the general area addressed by this finding?

Much knowledge   Little knowledge

1   2   (3)   4   5   6   7   8   9   10

3. To what degree does this finding correspond with your expectations?

Expected   Not expected

1   2   3   4   5   6   (7)   8   9   10

4. To what degree does this finding have immediate policy implications?

To a large extent   To a limited extent

(1)   2   3   4   5   6   7   8   9   10

5. Given that this finding accurately reflects reality, is it stated in a concise and clear fashion, i.e., does it communicate?

Communicates well   Communicates poorly

1   (2)   3   4   5   6   7   8   9   10

C. For a Finding Selected for Significant Policy Implications

1. What policy action(s) might be precipitated by this finding?

   a. *"Give no awards to the 'have' states. This is probably not a politically feasible option, however."*

   b. *"The program should be differentiated into two progams, i.e.:*

      (1) A capacity building grant program for states with weak to low dissemination systems already in operation; and

      (2) A supplementary dissemination grants program in states with more mature, established systems to support demonstration (for other states), dissemination across states, experimentation, and evaluation."

2. What further information would you need to modify policy or take action based on this finding? (What additional questions would you pose?)

   Information that would allow development of an activity appropriate to these 11 states to further their dissemination activities, since they don't need capacity building awards.

D. Finally, for the Leadership/Management Component:

Write in the space below a "finding statement" in this component that would support a recommendation on your part to drastically revamp the State Capacity Building Program.

"Data that activities run out of an Intermediate Service Agency (ISA) or decentralized information office are more successful than those centralized in and run by a State Education Agency (SEA)."

Linkages

A. Hypothetical Finding Statement

Only five of the 24 states employ full-time linking personnel funded through their own budget (or through budgets of intermediate units or LEAs). Full-time linking agents appear to provide better services than do those who perform a linkage function in addition to other functions. Most states use a combination of full- and part-time linkers. Part-time linkers serve more as a funnel for (prepackaged) information packages prepared within the resources component; full-time linkers perform transformations of information and work closely with the clients.

B. Guidelines (circle your response)

1. To what degree is this finding within the purview of the NTS evaluation?

Definitely within   Definitely without

1   (2)   3   4   5   6   7   8   9   10

2. How much knowledge do you have of the general area addressed by this finding?

Much knowledge   Little knowledge

1   2   3   (4)   5   6   7   8   9   10

3. To what degree does this finding correspond with your expectations?

Expected   Not expected

1   2   (3)   4   5   6   7   8   9   10

4. To what degree does this finding have immediate policy implications?

To a large extent   To a limited extent

1   2   (3)   4   5   6   7   8   9   10

5. Given that this finding accurately reflects reality, is it stated in a concise and clear fashion, i.e., does it communicate?

Communicates well   Communicates poorly

1   2   3   4   5   ⑥   7   8   9   10

C. For a Finding Selected for Significant Policy Implications

1. What policy action(s) might be precipitated by this finding?

   a. *"The policy implication is clear—hire more full-time agents—but it does not take account of resource constraints."*

2. What further information would you need to modify policy or take action based on this finding? (What additional questions would you pose?)

   "Information not specific enough to draw conclusions. Costs? In what way are the services provided 'better'? What 'better' results are obtained by working more closely with clients? Are the extra costs worth it?"

D. Finally, for the Linkage Component:

Write in the space below a "finding statement" in this component that would support a recommendation on your part to drastically revamp the State Capacity Building Program.

"Users prefer document-based information system at their immediate command and—where they have it—find it of greater utility."

"This finding would be so out of keeping with the basic premise of the Program that it (the Program) would have to be changed radically."

Information Resources

A. Hypothetical Finding Statement

Although all states subscribe to the notion that dissemination involves two-way communication and that the information base should evolve in response to user demand, it was found that in 20 of the states the nature of the information resource base was largely determined by SEA staff with little formal or informal assessment of user needs. Project staff said that political and economic exigencies dictated the scope of the information resource base.

B. Guidelines (circle your response)

1. To what degree is this finding within the purview of the NTS evaluation?

Definitely within   Definitely without

①   2   3   4   5   6   7   8   9   10

2. How much knowledge do you have of the general area addressed by this finding?

Much knowledge   Little knowledge

1   2   ③   4   5   6   7   8   9   10

3. To what degree does this finding correspond with your expectations?

Expected   Not expected

1   2   3   4   5   ⑥   7   8   9   10

4. To what degree does this finding have immediate policy implications?

To a large extent   To a limited extent

1   ②   3   4   5   6   7   8   9   10

5. Given that this finding accurately reflects reality, is it stated in a concise and clear fashion, i.e., does it communicate?

Communicates well   Communicates poorly

1   2   3   ④   5   6   7   8   9   10

C. For a Finding Selected for Significant Policy Implications

1. What policy action(s) might be precipitated by this finding?

   "Build needs assessment component into project."

2. What further information would you need to modify policy or take action based on this finding? (What additional questions would you pose?)

   "Validity of 'political/economic constraints' pleading."

   "Recommendations on how to perform useful needs assessment."

   "Recommendations on how SEAs would acquire greater credibility with teachers and LEA administrators."

D. Finally, for the Information Research Component:

Write in the space below a "finding statement" in this component that would support a recommendation on your part to drastically revamp the State Capacity Building Program.

   "Documented demand by users that they are seeking very different information from what they're getting. For example, in an SEA essentially using ERIC as its resource base, demand by teachers (say at a level of 30% or more of all teacher inquiries) that they get information on and actual samples of instructional materials (e.g., 2nd grade arithmetic series, 7th grade social studies for Chicano students)."

NOTES

1. For a more extensive description of the NIE-sponsored State Capacity Building Program and its evaluation, readers are referred to the five volumes prepared by NTS Research Corporation which comprise the final report. The complete set of volumes, each of which has the same general title, *Building Capacity for the Improvement of Educational Practice,* is as follows:

Volume I: An Evaluation of NIE's State Dissemination Grants Program: Final Evaluation Report (December 1980)
Volume II: 1979 State Abstracts: State Dissemination Efforts (October 1980)
Volume III: A Study of Linker Agent Activities and Roles (October 1980)
Volume IV: A Study of The Development of Scales Measuring Dissemination Capacity (December 1980)
Volume V: An Evaluation of NIE's State Dissemination Grants Program: Executive Summary (December 1980)

2. The evaluation was comprised of four phases: (1) a design phase (October 1976 - August 1977) devoted to describing the program; clarifying and translating the program's goals into measurable variables; and developing a design, appropriate instrumentation, and data collection and analysis procedures for the study; (2) a preparation period (September 1977 - August 1978) which included initial fieldwork in 23 project sites, some descriptive reporting, refinements in the study design, and approval of a forms clearance package; (3) a full-scale evaluation (September 1978 - April 1980) which included two waves of quantitative data collection (Fall 1978, in 33 project states; and Fall 1979, in all 50 states) and an additional wave of quantitative data collection (Winter 1980, in five project states); and (4) a dissemination phase (July 1980 - April 1981) in which the study's findings and implications were shared with policy makers, researchers, and practitioners.

REFERENCES

BAILEY, S. K. (1979) "Current educational policy analysis: an insight." Educational Evaluation and Policy Analysis 1 (March-April) 95-100.

BAKER, R. F., J. K. DECAD, E. C. ROYSTER, and D. L. MADEY (1980) Building Capacity for the Improvement of Educational Practice: Volume IV—A Study of the Development of Scales Measuring Dissemination Capacity. Report prepared for the National Institute of Education under Contract 400-76-0166. Durham, NC: NTS Research Corporation.

BERRYMAN, S. E. and T. K. GLENNAN (1980) "An improved strategy for evaluating federal programs in education," pp. 11-40 in J. Pincus (ed.) Educational Evaluation in the Public Policy Setting. Santa Monica, CA: Rand Corporation.

BISSELL, J. S. (1979) "Use of educational evaluation and policy studies." Educational Evaluation and Policy Analysis 1 (March-April) 29-37.

DECAD, J. K., D. L. MADEY, E. C. ROYSTER, and R. F. BAKER (1980) Building Capacity for the Improvement of Educational Practice: Volume III—A Study of Linker Agent Activities and Roles. Report prepared for the National Institute of Education under Contract 3400-76-0166. Durham, NC: NTS Research Corporation.

EVANS, J. (1969) "Evaluating social action programs." Social Science Quarterly 50,3: 586-581.

FILSTEAD, W. J. (1980) "The epistemology of social policy." Presented at the fourth annual meeting of the Evaluation Research Society, November.

GIDEONSE, H. D. (1980) "Improving the federal administration of education programs." Educational Evaluation and Policy Analysis 2 (January-February) 61-70.

HAYMAN, J., N. RAYDER, A. J. STENNER, and D. L. MADEY (1979) "On aggregation, generalization, and utility in educational evaluation." Educational Evaluation and Policy Analysis 1 (July-August) 31-39.

HILL, P. T. (1980) "Evaluating education programs for federal policymakers: lessons from the NIE compensatory education study," pp. 48-76 in J. Pincus (ed.) Educational Evaluation in the Public Policy Setting. Santa Monica, CA: Rand Corporation.

KAHN, H. and A. J. WIENER (1967) The Year 2000, A framework for Speculation on the Next Thirty-Three Years. New York: MacMillan.

MADEY, D. L. (1981) "Some benefits of integrating qualitative and quantitative methods in program evaluation, with illustrations." Educational Evaluation and Policy Analysis.

——— (1980) Building Capacity for the Improvement of Educational Practice: Volume II—1979 State Abstracts, State Dissemination Efforts. Report prepared for the National Institute of Education under Contract 400-76-0166. Durham, NC: NTS Research Corporation.

——— E.C. ROYSTER, J. K. DECAD, and R. F. BAKER (1980) Building Capacity for the Improvement of Educational Practice: Volume I—An Evaluation of NIE's State Dissemination Grants Program (Final Evaluation Report). Report prepared for the National Institute of Education under Contract 400-76-0166. Durham, NC: NTS Research Corporation.

MASON, W. S. (1973) Problems of Measurement and the NIE Program. Washington, DC: National Institute of Education.

McNEIL, J. T., R. ROSANTE-LORO, J. WEDELL-MONNIG, K. WATTERSON, and M. SZEGDA (1980) Description and Analysis of Program Data: Head Start Sample Programs (National Evaluation of Head Start Educational Services and Basic Educational Skills Demonstration Programs, Project Report 7). Durham, NC: NTS Research Corporation.

PATTON, M. Q. (1978) Utilization-Focused Evaluation. Beverly Hills, CA: Sage.

PINCUS, J. [ed.] (1980) Educational Evaluation in the Public Policy Setting. Santa Monica, CA: Rand Corporation.

ROSS, L. and L. J. CRONBACH [eds.] (1976) "Handbook of evaluation research." Educational Researcher 5 (November): 9-19.

ROYSTER, E. C., D. L. MADEY, J. K. DECAD, and R. F. BAKER (1980) Building Capacity for the Improvement of Educational Practice: An Evaluation of NIE's State Dissemination Grants Program: Volume V—Executive Summary. Report prepared for the National Institute of Education under Contract 400-76-0166. Durham, NC: NTS Research Corporation.

SCRIVEN, M. (1974) "Evaluation perspectives and procedures," pp. 1-93 in W. J. Popham (ed.) Evaluation in Education. Berkeley, CA: McCutchan Publishing Corp.

SMITH, N. L. (1980) "Federal research on evaluation methods in health, criminal justice and the military." Educational Evaluation and Policy Analysis 2 (July-August): 53-59.

STENNER, A. J. (1974) An Overview of Information Based Evaluation: A Design Procedure, Information Based Evaluation Series, Book 1. Durham, NC: IBEX.

STENNER, A. J. and D. L. MADEY (1976) Policy Implications Analysis, Exercise 1: "Design for the evaluation of the state capacity building program in dissemination." Durham, NC: NTS Research Corporation.

STUFFLEBEAM, D. L. (1974) "Alternative approaches to educational evaluation: A self-study guide for educators," pp. 95-144 in W. J. Popham (ed.) Evaluation in Education. Washington, DC: American Educational Research Association.

WEILER, D. and M. STEARNS (1980) "The uses and limits of educational evaluation at the state level," pp. 77-85 in J. Pincus (ed.) Educational Evaluation in the Public Policy Setting. Santa Monica, CA: Rand Corporation.

WEISS, C. H. (1977) Using Social Research in Public Policymaking. Lexington, MA: Lexington Books.

3

Robert F. Boruch
Northwestern University

RANDOMIZED EXPERIMENTS AT NATIONAL, STATE, AND LOCAL LEVELS OF GOVERNMENT:
Recommendations from a Report to Congress

INTRODUCTION

In the fourth century B.C., the philosopher Democritus asserted that he would rather uncover a single causal connection than sit on the throne of Persia. It is not clear that policy makers can or should have the same preference, especially if the choice of thrones is enlarged a bit. It is clear that the two aspirations are not incompatible, and this chapter is addressed partly to their limited union.

The special focus is a report submitted in 1980 by a group at Northwestern University to the Congress and the U.S. Department of Education. Mandated under the 1978 Educational Amendments, the study on which it is based reviewed evaluations of federally supported education programs at the national, state, and local levels of government.[1] Congresswoman Elizabeth Holtzman of New York introduced the bill that required the study. Her interest lay in understanding the product of the government's $30 to $40 million an-

AUTHOR'S NOTE: Background research for this chapter has been supported by the National Institute of Education (Grant NIE-G-79-0129) and the National Science Foundation (NSF-DAR-7820374). The Holtzman project was supported in 1980-1981 by OED-300-79-0467, and its conception was influenced considerably by John Evans and Marshall Smith. The paper extends and updates one that appears in the *American Statistician*. The journal's referees for this paper were generous in providing advice on its improvement, and I am grateful to them.

nual investment in educational evaluation. The enterprise was designed, then, to answer questions about why evaluations are undertaken by government, who does them, how well they are done, and how the results of evaluation are used. A parallel report, commissioned later, has been issued by the National Academy of Sciences Committee on Program Evaluation (Raizen and Rossi, 1981).

Northwestern's report considers a number of problems in this arena, not the least being lexical promiscuity. A federal director of research, for instance, announced that he did no evaluations, and fifteen minutes later his superior, a deputy secretary, informed us that everything in his shop was evaluation.[2] Here, for clarity's sake, evaluation is defined as attempts to answer one or more of the following questions: Who needs services and who receives them? What is the nature and cost of services? What are the effects of service? What are the costs and benefits of alternatives? Such questions are apropos for programs aside from education, of course, and so this chapter exploits the products of applied research in welfare, medicine, crime, and other areas as well.

This chapter focuses on one aspect of the report, notably the recommendations on evaluation designs, especially randomized experiments, in estimating the effects of education programs. Experiments here include settings in which children, classrooms, or entire school districts are randomly assigned to one, two, or more methods of improving education, in order to estimate their relative costs or effects fairly and to make probabilistic statements about the result. The design is sturdy in the sense that the logic is plain, albeit deceptively so, robust and well thought out. But as many readers know, it can be difficult to use outside the laboratory. And, as perhaps fewer realize, the design usually reduces ambiguity in a notable way, but does not and cannot eliminate it.

The concern about randomized field tests is not unique in that Rivlin (1971), Riecken et al. (1974), Gilbert, Light, and Mosteller (1977), and others have considered its role in public policy. Fisher, too, seems to have shipped in these waters to judge from Cochran's (1976) review of the Lanakshire trial on provision of milk to schoolchildren. The concern is distinctive in that I am aware of few reports to the Congress that deal with the topic at all, much less at federal, state, and local levels of government. Still fewer deal with experiments in the broad context of program evaluation policy.

THE RECOMMENDATION TO THE DEPARTMENT AND TO CONGRESS

The report made seven broad recommendations to the Department and to the Congress. The recommendation to each, bearing on experiments, was:

> Good evaluation designs...are not used often, partly because innovations are planned independent of evaluation. We recommend that pilot tests be undertaken before new programs or new variations are adopted and that the introduction of new programs be staged so that good designs can be exploited. Further, we recommend that higher quality evaluation designs, especially randomized experiments, be authorized explicitly in law for testing new programs, new variation on existing programs, and new program components.

The rationale for suggesting pilot tests in education is not much different from medicine, energy consumption, income subsidy, and other areas. We believe that such tests are more feasible and more useful before a program is adopted at any level of government. Moreover, better evaluation designs can be employed, conclusions are less likely to be ambiguous, and political-institutional constraints on design are less likely to be severe before the program is implemented on a large scale.

This suggestion is terribly simple, even mundane. But recognize that in recent political discussion of the proposed Youth Incentives Program, for instance, an enterprise whose costs could exceed $850 million per year, there has been no formal attention to pilot testing or staged introduction of the program. The Title I compensatory education program evolved with little real testing ten years ago. What is know about its effects is still meager on that account. Reiterating the notion that massive new programs, or for that matter major new budget cuts, ought to be pilot tested seems to be warranted simply because it is not yet a common practice.

The second part of the recommendation uses "authorization" as a vehicle for higher quality designs. By this I mean explicit and official permission. I do *not* mean that such designs should be required uniformly, for such a demand is absurd. The distinction is subtle, but as Bunda's (1981) criticism of the Holtzman report implies, it is crucial. Nor is the recommendation meant to imply that randomized tests are the only option in many settings. Other designs, including those that address questions different from outcome, are often important. The general suggestion is based on the presumption that we will not learn how to bring about detectable change in the performance of children or schools without more conscientiously designed tests. Its justification lies partly in the poor quality of designs used in the field. It is distressingly easy to find, for example, testimony being offered to congressional committees by a state legislator, declaring that a Title I compensatory education program is a success because "test scores went up." Very little attention is dedicated at the local level to competing explanations for gains in achievement, such as, normal growth apart from special programs. A kind of benign hypocrisy characterizes the business: gains are attributed to the program publicly, but privately there is some admission of doubt. The same is *not* true for many if not all recent major federal evaluations of effect, however, and for a minority of the evaluations produced at the school district level. Many have been blunt and candid in reporting and conscientious in describing plausible competing explanations.

There are several reasons for suggesting explicit statutory provisions that permit randomized designs. First, such tests are best in principle when the objective is to estimate relative differences, the standard of evidence is reasonably high, and prior theory on the program is weak. The merit of tests under these common conditions ought to be publicly recognized. More important, it is reasonable to expect authorization will expand the local and state evaluator's ability to undertake good tests of new federally sponsored programs. This local leverage is important given lay disinterest in or opposition to balanced evidence. For the federal agency that must meet congressional or management demands for impact information on a larger scale, authorization makes it clear that experiments are a legitimate option, if not always the preferred one, and it can help to secure the cooperation of local and state officials in multisite trials.

FEASIBILITY AND APPROPRIATENESS

The usefulness of randomized tests in principle is generally not an issue in professional discussion about evaluating new education programs. There is agreement that when experiments are conducted properly, orthodox theory guarantees that estimates of effects will be unbiased. The conditions under which they can or should be employed is more debatable. Pincus et al. (1981) and Cronbach (1980) offer conditions that differ a bit from the ones discussed here, and efforts to understand points of disagreement are underway.

Precedent

Some arguments concern the idea that randomized experiments are rarely feasible in field settings. Rareness and feasibility are, however, infrequently specified by government policy groups or by individual analysts. The novelty of the idea in social research does not establish lack of feasibility and a notable, if not large, number of field tests have been mounted. The most recent examples include national evaluations of parts of the Emergency School Aid Act; local evaluations of career education programs supported by the National Institute of Education; Middle Start programs tested at Oberlin College for high school students; preschool educational television programs, such as *Feeling Good* and *Sesame Street,* that were tested regionally; and even grade retention. Randomized tests of radio-based mathematics instruction in Nicaragua, of educational enrichment in Colombia, and of tutoring programs in Israel (Davis, 1981) are exemplars outside the United States (Boruch et al., 1978). Judging from precedent, then, bald claims that it is impossible to assign individuals randomly to programs for the sake of fair estimates of program effects are unwarranted. Experiments *are* in the minority though, and perhaps this is due to constraints on their feasibility and appropriateness, considered below.

Pilot Tests of Randomized Experiments

Precedent is persuasive only in the crudest sense. It implies that what has been done might be done again—but it may be immaterial to the situation at hand. For this reason, pilot tests of large-scale field experiments are worth considering. That is, small experiments prior to the main experiment can yield more direct evidence on feasibility than history can offer, and can identify problems before the main effort. That there are many problems in mounting randomized tests is clear. For instance, some 50 randomized tests of Head Start programs were initiated recently, despite counsel for more pilot work; less than ten succeeded. In tighter tests, two of six experiments on bilingual bicultural education appear to have been implemented successfully since 1976 (Chavez et al., 1981), and the Agency for Children, Youth, and Families deserves applause for getting these off the ground as a considerable improvement over earlier work by others.

Experiments fail to be successfully implemented in education as in medicine, law enforcement, and other areas because the randomization is corrupted, because the programs are not implemented as advertised, and because of attrition and other reasons. The practice of pilot-testing field test strategy, or more informally scouting the terrain for better opportunities for such tests, seems uncommon. Yet there are good precedents elsewhere that approach regular pilots of the sort I have in mind. These include small randomized tests of alternative methods for eliciting information in new health surveys. They include designing experiments sequentially so that early experiments serve as a test bed on which later experiments can improve, as in the negative income tax experiments in New Jersey during the early 1970s and in Seattle and Denver during the late 1970s (Robins and West, 1981), and as in Oberlin College's sequence of tests of Middle Start programs for promising high school students. They include small scale local experiments designed to anticipate larger scale statewide experiments in administrative law, for example (Corsi and Hurley, 1979).

Appropriateness and Feasibility: Conditions

Precedent will not always be available to guide decisions about experiments, and there will often be little time for pilot work. So it is reasonable to educe general conditions under which experiments might be mounted. The earlier remarks stress that new programs are more compatible with randomized testing than existing ones, and setting this as a heuristic condition seems reasonable. Others are as important and more fundamental.

Information Needs. There is not much point to investing scarce evaluation resources in an experiment if no one is interested in the result. The disinterest may apply to *any* evidence about outcome, a not-uncommon characteristic of social program development. It may be born of opposition ("Don't ask if you don't want the answer"), especially in regard to negative and positive effects of dismantling a program. The opposition may also be reasonable in that no major decisions can be made on the basis of such data. It may also be sensible in that approaches other than experiments, though they yield more ambiguous information, are sufficient for making crude decisions.

Perhaps most important, other policy questions may take precedence over estimation of effects: Do those who need service get it? Are the services sensible relative to standards of an expert judge and are they delivered? And so on. The fundamental issue of what questions should be asked and are answerable was addressed in the Holtzman report in the content and in several recommendations. Criticisms leveled against the report on this count by Bunda (1981) and House (1980) stress these alternatives rather than questions about effect; and independent reports, such as Pincus et al. (1980), suggest that such questions are far more frequently asked and, therefore, are more important than questions about effect. Most school districts with research offices, for example, appear not to be concerned with estimating the relative costs and benefits of alternative programs, if we judge by UCLA's recent survey of offices' activity (Lyon et al., 1978). Yet there are remarkable exceptions at the local level, such as Rickel et al.'s (1979) tests on mental health programs and the Middle Start experiments cited earlier. Estimating effects of programs and of costs and benefits of alternatives appears to be of rather more concern to the federal government, if we judge by the fraction of projects with this purpose supported by the Office of Evaluation at the Department of Education (Boruch and Cordray, forthcoming). But the majority of projects address questions other than those on effect.

The point is that experimental results may be less useful and less important than other information. I believe it depends on the particular case and level of government. Recognizing and making explicit the choices are usually not easy, especially where the public and its representatives have an active voice in the design of an evaluation, as they often do.

Randomization, Equity, and Mechanics. Where there is an oversupply of eligible recipients for scarce program services, randomized assignment of candidates for the resource seems fair. So, for instance, Vancouver's Crisis Intervention Program for youthful offenders afforded equal opportunity to eligible recipients. According to Patricia Anderson (director of Vancouver's Health in Welfare Planning Council), since all could not be accommodated well with available program resources, but all were equally eligible, they were randomly assigned to program or control conditions. Scholars such as

Cook and Campbell (1979) argue that randomized experiments are most likely to be carried out successfully when the boon, real or imagined, is in short supply, and the demand for the boon is high. This rationale dovetails neatly with some managerial constraints. That is, new programs cannot be emplaced all at once despite the aspirations of program advocates. This argument is not especially useful, of course, when the manager can simply spread resources more thinly, for example, by expanding the size of classes dedicated to special instruction.

The same rationale also fits *some* legislative views of the way scarce resources may be allocated, but not others. The Emergency School Assistance Act and the field experiments it produced, for instance, appear to have been generated partly from the idea that the fair way to provide very little money to schools interested in developing desegregation programs was to distribute it randomly. Berger (forthcoming) provides evidence, in the form of judicial decisions, that the courts have "deferred" to such legislation, but in general the legitimacy of randomized distribution of resources depends on the funciton of distribution. If the purpose is to meet special needs rather than meet needs and produce scientific knowledge, other forms of distribution may be warranted.

The mechanics of randomization are, of course, no less important than its rationale. The key to avoiding subversion of the process in education as in medicine, meteorology, and other areas seems to be complete control of a blind randomization process and prior agreements about exceptions and adherence to the result (Conner, 1977). Neither is easy to obtain in educational settings. Yet studies, such as Conner's, that describe how randomization failed are still rare. It is more disappointing that the arguments, evidence, and methods used to get randomization accepted and accomplished are often *not* described well in published results of field tests. The same problem affects medical field experts, and it is partly for this reason that Mosteller, Gilbert, and McPeek (1980) encourage medical journal editors to require pertinent information in the articles they accept for publication. Their recommendation has some precedent in the U.S. General Accounting Office (1978) guidelines for assessing impact evaluations: information about how individuals were selected and assigned to programs is labeled as desirable.

New Variations and Components. For political and other reasons, it is inappropriate at times to compare a program, especially a popular one, to no program at all. A "no program control" condition may be pointless anyway if having no program after a test is an unacceptable political option. In such cases, it still makes sense to consider comparing the main program to variations or to test components. There are, of course, a fair number of illustrations. At the regional level, for example, randomized tests of cheap nondirective counseling and of small college course subsidies have been executed in the Seattle and Denver Income maintenance Experiments to discover their effect on earnings (Dickinson and West, 1981).

The idea of testing new variations or components rather than testing a program against a control condition is a compromise, perhaps a cowardly one. But getting some decent information on a subordinate question, such as which variation or component works better or more cheaply, is better than getting no information at all on the main one—what the effects are of the program. The strategy is not common in any agency, except perhaps that which periodically supports randomized tests to better understand methods of doing surveys.

Law. Little has been written by legal scholars on the legality of randomized field tests, partly because they know so little about the topic. But this is changing, too. For instance, the Federal Judicial Center, the research arm of the Supreme Court, created a Committee on Social Experimentation designed to explicate the posture that judges can take in looking at experimental tests of the effectiveness of judicial changes (Re, 1981).

Breger's (forthcoming) examination of the legal aspects of social experiments is applicable to research in mental health, energy, education, and a variety of areas and is the most thorough to date. He reviews federal statutes that empower federal administrative agencies to undertake randomized experiments, including explicit mandates (such as the Emergency School Assistance Act that lead to randomized tests) and less explicit law (such as waiver authority that is necessary to manipulate regulation or procedures in field tests). Breger also reviews pertinent court decisions. For example, in *Aguayo v. Richardson* and *California Welfare Rights Organization v. Richardson,* the use of randomized experiments in assessing the welfare programs was challenged, and the challenges were dismissed by the court. Institutional Review Boards, required for research supported by both the Department of Human Services and the Department of Education, are also pertinent; and Breger examines their role in assaying risks and benefits of experimentation. One of the remarkable aspects of that role is Board review of the adequacy of an experiment's design. That is, a project based on poor design will not meet a Board "test of risk benefit comparison because it cannot provide scientifically legitimate knowledge" and the court can incorporate the judgment into its own decision about the legitimacy of demonstrations, quasi-experiments, and randomized field tests.

Statutes that explicitly recognize the legitimacy of randomized experiments, as an option, are still rather scarce, however. And this is one of the reasons for recommending explicit law in the Holtzman report.

Statistical Matters. The conventional statistical issues are as pertinent in formal tests of education projects as they are in other settings. These considerations include sample size and power, the unit of randomization and of analysis, additivity of effects and multiplicity of response variables, and so on. These can be as problematic in social experimentations as they are in experiments in, say, chemical engineering and agriculture, and often they are much more complex and less tractable. The point to considering such issues here is they can rarely be treated well when a legal demand for evaluation is enacted. The law must permit the time necessary for planning initiation and termination of experiments for technical reasons. Assuring this flexibility is one objective of the recommendations considered below, notably those that ask the Congress and the Department to allocate sufficient time, before or after enactment of law, to clarifying the objectives, feasibility, and appropriateness of evaluation that is required by the statute.

OTHER RECOMMENDATIONS

Several other recommendations in the report bear directly on higher quality field tests. The Congress was urged to be more direct in its demands for information *when directness is possible.* In particular, we suggested that laws request information about *who* is served, *need* for service, *nature* of service, and/or *effect* of service, rather than just asking for an "evaluation." This was coupled with a recommendation to allocate time for regular discussion between agency and congressional staffs with evaluation responsibility, to clarify the questions gradually, and identify the answerable ones. One rationale for this is assuring that outcome evaluations are specified clearly and that their difficulty is well understood.

A related recommendation suggested that audiences for evaluation results be identified beforehand if possible and, moreover, that some resources be invested in research on how information can be better used. The idea is to help assure that evaluators can understand their clients' interests. Congress must understand that information needed for the national level may be perfectly useless at the local level. Partly because some local and state agencies are capable of mounting good field tests on the effect of reducing information demands, of presenting information in more useful ways, and so on, the suggestion for competitive grants for such tests was tied to those levels of government.

The report also called for a routine *balanced* critique of major federal program evaluations and periodic critique of a sample of locally conducted evaluations. A rationale for this was to facilitate identifying good and poor quality evaluations as such and to encourage better quality tests. The worst of the poor reports are ghastly. For instance, we found some local school district reports announcing dozens of F ratios of 9000 or more, references to t tests as being "convenient because their mean is 10 and variance 20," to ".001 level of significance as the highest probability one could achieve" in a statistical test, and so on. The recommendation to apply better methods will not help here; however, critiques, better training, and technical assistance might.

A third recommendation asked that evaluation capabilities at the local and state levels be assayed *before* new evaluation demands are imposed in federal regulations. It was based on the finding that capabilities and demands vary considerably. To the extent that evaluations involve estimating program effects, for instance, the expertise required by such evaluation ought to be recognized. Pleas of incompetence may be coated with a veneer of active hostility and plain indifference; this does not make the plea any less legitimate. A related recommendation to provide technical assistance is predicated on capability assessments. Though it is focused on local and state agencies, this suggestion now may apply to some federal operating agencies as well. For instance, the creation of a Department of Education and internal management changes have been accompanied by a loss of some good evaluation staff.

One of the recommendations urges the Congress *not* to adopt uniform evalution standards in law. Our objective was to prevent inflexible application of rules that change as the state of the art develops. The report does encourage adherence to sensible guidelines by agency staff with pertinent training. This recommendation is compatible with the one of using higher quality designs in that, although we advocate the latter, there is no suggestion that they are always warranted as law might be interpreted to imply. Relevant guidelines have been produced, for example, by the U.S. General Accounting Office (1978) and by independent professional organizations. The GAO guidelines on judging impact evaluation reports, incidentally, are similar in some respects to those offered by Mosteller, Gilbert, and McPeek (1980) to editors of medical journals on the publication of reports from clinical trials. Such efforts, reviewed in the Holtzman Report, are likely to be useful in screening projects at the local and state, as well as federal, levels of governance.

A final recommendation, made to the Department rather than the Congress, urged that more attention be given the problem of assessing the level of implementation of programs. There is not much point, for example, in mounting a randomized test at the local, regional, or national level if one cannot verify that the program has been emplaced as designed. And partial implementation complicates matters no end (see the next section). The problems of assessment occurs in small local tests as well as in large-scale experiments (Boruch and Wortman, 1979; Chavez et al., 1981). The specific advice was to invest more research money into learning how to better assay implementation and more administrative resources in understanding cheap devices for monitoring and consolidating data about implementation.

APPLICATIONS FOR THE STATISTICIAN AND METHODOLOGIST

Judging from our own work and from others', several aspects of educational field experiments deserve much more attention from statisticians. These affect experiments in other social settings, of course. (See Mosteller, Gilbert, and McPeek, 1980, for a different selection.)

Design Power and Integrity of Treatment Response

The transfer of statistical methods across substantive areas often engenders new and interesting problems. These problems, not treated in texts such as Fisher's, Kempthorne's, Cox's, or other classics, include the fact that treatments are rarely delivered as advertised, that they are not "fixed" in the same sense that treatments are fixed in the chemical sciences or biology, and that response variables are measured poorly or are irrelevant to the treatment. Recent work, for example, suggests that statistical power in field tests can drop badly with moderate degradation of the integrity of treatment delivery and the quality in measurement of response. Where simple linear models are used to represent integrity of each in power computations and integrity is reduced by 25 percent, power drops to only a third of the value it might be expected to take in laboratory settings (Boruch and Gomez, 1979). This multiplicative decline in power can occur in testing programs in criminal justice (Sechrest and Redner, 1979), economic subsidy, health services delivery, and elsewhere. Though they may be more severe in these areas, the problems have also occurred in experiments on weather modification, agriculture, and medicine. The difficulty is pervasive in education, judging from results of both small and large scale experiments (Boruch and Wortman, 1979). As such, it deserves more attention from able statisticians to identify stereotypical ways in which treatment integrity can be degraded, to represent them mathematically, and to educe their implications for power and products of field tests.

It is also important that response variables are often measured on scales which do *not* have (roughly speaking) equal intervals, and so estimates of program effect may be biased by a high floor or low ceiling on the scale of measurement. The problem is especially severe in nonrandomized tests where changes in reliability of measurement of achievement (say) and differences in reliability across a group complicate matters further. But it can deflate estimates in randomized tests as well, and make long-term longitudinal studies of child development difficult (Campbell and Boruch, 1975). Accommodating stereotypical forms of corruption of measurement in social experiments has received attention only recently from the statistician, for example, randomized response, dual system estimates, and probabilistic approaches to detection of cheating. There is a need for inventing new technology in a similar spirit for evaluative settings that are especially susceptible to indifference, incompetence, and corruption. The point is that there are important measurement problems which have not been well articulated in the orthodox literature in randomized experiments. Bringing randomized design into the social program evaluation area means we have to solve these problems and this may lead to technical innovation.

Nonrandom Tests When Assignment is Prescribed

Twenty years ago, Donald T. Campbell formally proposed that one could generate reasonable estimates of program effect if selection to a program was based on measurable criterion rather than on randomization. In the simplest case, one knows there is a linear relation between a continuous response variable and the continuous measure of need or merit for program services. One then assigns individuals to services in accord with a cutting point that separates the needy from the others. The estimate of effect is based on the difference, in elevation, say, between two regressions of response on the selection measure, one above and one below the cutting point (Chapter 4 of Riecken et al., 1974). In principle, the design solves a major specification problem, and the statistical analysis has been worked out for the simple cases. The idea of selection based on need rather than randomization is also nominally more attractive to some program developers. In practice, though, the form of the curve under null conditions must often be guessed; both response and selection variables are fallible and may be measured on scales whose units are unequal, especially at extremes; treatment effect may be nonadditive; and assignment is likely to be badly mangled at the cutting point. The statistical problems have not been well explored though there are fragments. Moreover, the design is being used; the problems are being used; the problems are being identified better in, among others, local school district estimates of the effect of Title I compensatory education programs (Trochim and Spiegelman, 1981). Because these are influenced by federal and state regulations, it is possible for the statistician to mount good investigations of the technique. Such investigations are important in that the idea can be exploited in federal statistical policy to use formula allocation laws not only for allocating resources but also for estimating the impact of those resources.

Coupling Randomized Experiments and Nonrandomized Tests

The technology of designing randomized tests has not developed independent of the technology of nonrandomized tests such as quasi-experiments or time series analysis. Yet disciplinary separation is often sufficient to prevent statisticians from thinking about both in the design of evaluations. Nonetheless, there are good reasons for coupling approaches when the opportunity arises.

Part of our suspicion of nonrandomized tests, for example, is based on our ignorance about misspecification and competing explanations for what caused the effect. Some of the suspicion is warranted in that when we compare estimates based on randomized trials and those based on nonrandomized ones, the results differ. Some may be unwarranted but difficult to dispel because a priori or a posteriori results do not differ, and there is not much chance of coming to agreement without common evidence (see Boruch, 1976, for references). The issue is old, too—Fisher and Gosset appear to have locked horns over the matter (Box's [1981] description of this and other exchanges is fascinating).

So it does not seem unreasonable to design simultaneous randomized and nonrandomized field tests to gradually accumulate empirical estimates of bias in nonrandomized tests. Such information can be critical for future evaluations in which randomization is not possible. Illustrations of the approach have been forced by circumstance rather than by interest in comparison. The Salk polio vaccine trials, for example, accommodated state prerogatives by setting up a randomized design and one kind of nonrandomized design in parallel. The benefit of combination can be heuristic: experiments become test beds for nonexperimental designs, and the information that accumulates from such trials can be synthesized periodically to help decide when and if quasi-experiments can substitute for randomized trials. The benefit of combination in other cases is likely to be better estimates of effect. That is, estimates based on a few expensive randomized tests and a larger group of cheaper nonrandomized tests might be combined using regression estimators in the interest of obtaining both accuracy and precision in a multisite trial (Boruch, 1975). Similarly, benefit may accrue from the fact that some quasi-experimental designs can yield less equivocal estimates of program effects than an experiment that fails due to unspecifiable attrition. A technology of contingency designs does not yet exist, and it should.

In still other settings, coupling analyses of variance based on the randomized design and structural models based on the design and other information will be illuminating. The state of the art in such unions is still developing and warrants more attention. So for instance, Rossi, Berk, and Lenihan's (1980: 93) analysis of variance of data from experimental tests of parole subsidy programs suggested that the effect of subsidy on property crimes was negligible. They built on economic theory, evidence, and common sense to construct structural models that suggest that the number of property crimes is typically reduced (Rossi et al., 1980: 239). The debate over this conflict continues. There will probably be less debate over the analysis of variance and parallel structural model analysis of data from the Seattle and Denver Income Maintenance Experiments. In these, economic theory is exploited in the structural models, the experimental data being used to verify direction and nature of changes in wage rate and other variables; and there is a closer correspondence between the two approaches. How much more can be said by combining the two is a legitimate question for the field experimenter, methodologist, and the substantive theoretician.

Finally, it is not clear whether and how to design for sequential trials in which randomized tests alternate with nonrandom tests in the interest of accommodating guinea pig effects and other problems induced perhaps by randomized experiments but not by nonrandomized tests. It is not clear how one ought to design simultaneous randomized and nonrandomized trials in anticipation of internal analyses that must ignore the randomization category at least partly, but which are also used to inform policy. Nor is it clear how to decide whether combining estimates of effect is warranted and how to combine, when confronted with a set of independent randomized and nonrandomized field tests, a problem which Pillemer and Light (1979) are assaulting for the case of randomized experiments.

Design for Early, Interim, and Late Results

Experiments depend heavily on program planners' willingness to wait for results before initiating program changes, since stability is required. The analyst's interest in stability is understandable. But the changes that usually occur imply that several other options ought to be examined.

The impatience implied here, for example, is a two-way street. To the extent that it is in some measure justified and persistent, one may argue that, as research designers, we should develop plans which *always* provide supplementary information early in a long-term study and perhaps better administrative information during the exercise; that we be able to identify changes that occur in midstream and that theoretically have no notable effect on outcome in the experiment. It also seems sensible to develop technique for anticipating changes whose effects are unlikely to be negligible and for adjoining small tests to those changes in the interest of estimation. More generally, it behooves us to invent operating theory to cover the need for information during an experiment rather than only after the experiment's termination. We have no such theory now, though the state of the art is developing.

The other side of this street concerns unwarranted impatience. Many educational and social problems are chronic. They are resolved in small steps over a long period despite innovative social programs dedicated to their elimination and inspirational rhetoric. For these and other reasons (Zweig and Marvin, 1981), state legislatures and the Congress need to be reminded discreetly about ingenuous expectations. Some legislators *are* educable in this respect; some legislative assistants are well informed and thoughtful about the matter. How we get the education done for the other clients is not clear. But legislative committee structures, such as Wisconsin's, which facilitate the inclusion of Ph.D.-level researchers as members are a promising vehicle for this task. At the local level, only a few school boards have such expertise, but even here inclusion can be productive if we judge from the very few examples available, for example, in Arlington, Virginia. High turnover of legislative staff, legislators, and some executives make the need chronic at other levels of governance.

Cost-Benefit Analysis of Experiments

The absence of formal cost-benefit analyses of evaluations, including experiments, is remarkable. Part of the problem lies in defining benefits. These are often not clear unless the evaluation results are used, and "use" is typically not well documented and understood. An experiment's finding that a new program was unsuccessful, for instance, might imply an increased budget so as to salvage a product in public demand, or a decreased budget in the interest of reallocating resources to more promising projects. This implies a risk of defining use and benefit so broadly as to make it meaningless. Narrow definitions of use are equally misleading. Some reports appear to be influential in shaping attitudes and understanding, though they cannot be linked to specific decisions. The difficulty of specifying political decision options beforehand exacerbates the problem of linking information to action. There are a few good illustrations of orderly accounting of costs and benefits in day care and fertility control. No theoretical treatment analogous to Spencer's (1980) benefit cost analysis of data used to allocate funds appears to have been produced. The illustrations suggest that there is, indeed, a class of evaluations that is amenable to cost-benefit analysis, but more serious attention is warranted.

Appropriate Technology

During the thirteenth century, an extended rabbinic dialog concerned whether one should take a systematic sample or be content with an opportunistic or "convenience" sample as a basis for determining the value of a crop, the cost of each approach being very different. The resolution was that, in such cases, the level of quality that is warranted depends on the user of the information. If the demand for information is biblical in origin—if God wants it—the information ought to be precise; if rabbinic, one could be satisfied with an opportunistic approach (Rabinovitch, 1973).

The argument is pertinent to evaluation, of course. A manager may, for example, be satisfied with a census of institutionalized children that is only 70 percent complete, because in observing that (say) 50 percent of the group has a specific handicap, it is possible to put algebraic bounds on its true relative incidence of 35-65 percent. This is crude to be sure, but adequate for many purposes. Similarly, one might be satisfied with an estimate of program effect that contained bias of unknown magnitude, so long as its lower and upper bounds could be realistically guessed, and especially where any more sophisticated experiment would be considerably more demanding and just as temporary in value as the "poorer" estimate. Work on the order of magnitude estimates, for instance, is consistent with this, but seems not to have progressed far. The topic includes the business of learning how to do cost-benefit analysis of information and of building a design sequence that permits falling back to a less desirable design in a controlled way rather than a post facto way when primary designs fail.

The topic also includes understanding how to improve design and management of small, fast turnaround case studies that exploit as much information as possible on project performance, recognizing that estimates of effect are impossible or terribly ambiguous. The technique for doing such studies is not yet well articulated in the literature. But a fair number of remarkable sets of cases have appeared as a result of demands for quick information. These include the production of evaluation reports, directed by Robert Berg at the Agency for International Development, bearing on projects in developing countries. They include analogous products of the Office of Inspector General (Hendricks, forthcoming) and the U.S. General Accounting Office. These merit the attention of the methodologist and serious review because they are a fundamental approach to understanding how to reason from mixtures of sometimes poor information.

The point is that the idea of appropriate technology is as pertinent in field evaluations as it is in engineering. The rabbinic argument suggests that the problem is old, and that rules can be developed to guide its resolution. I do not mean to imply here that good, less expensive technology is employed as often as it can be. Censuses are often taken, disguised as administrative reporting in educational evaluation reporting systems, for example, when samples of reports would arguably suffice (Datta, 1979). Rather, this is a plea for more assistance on how to reason from data that satisfy policy interests, but do not necessarily satisfy scientific standards. The tension between purists and pragmatists here is a persistent one in any human enterprise. It deserves more attention than it has received from the able methodologist and statistician.

Parochialism and Statistical Methods

The statistician's normal focus is on *statistical* methods, and that is fine. But it is reasonable to argue that statisticians have a responsibility to recognize that in order to use good statistical methods, one also may have to develop better methods of other kinds.

For example, the Social Science Research Council's Committee on Social Experimentation (Riecken et al., 1974) stressed several classes of problems in this arena, only one of which was statistical. The others include management problems, notably getting better judgments about the pool of units eligible and available for randomization, inventing alternative methods of making randomization more attractive or less unpalatable, choosing feasible times and units, and controlling and tracking randomization. They include political institutional difficulties—building policy, law, or regulation to understand when tests are warranted; facilitating better tests; understanding the way organizations can be used to foster those tests; and so on. The difficulties include ethical ones, including inventing devices that assist the evaluator in reporting with integrity and independence to sometimes hostile audiences. The idea here is that any one of these problems can affect the quality of "technically" well-designed experiments. And it seems sensible to develop a battery of managerial, statutory, and procedural solutions to each so as to encourage the use of good methods. Inventing different kinds of solutions to a given problem is not an especially unique notion, but it is important and has not been pursued with much vigor in this arena.

The parochialism has a historical tone. Stereotypical forms of corruption of measurement and its effect on policy has not received much attention despite recognition by Ibn Khaldun among others, as early as the fourteenth century, of the distortive influences on military reporting, demography, and the like. The Lanakshire trial appears to have been degraded by teachers who did not adhere to the assigned treatment regimen, a problem that occurs in similar ways in education, medicine, and social welfare experiments. Despite its prevalence, it receives little serious examination in important statistical texts.

The problem of understanding the merits of qualitative and quantitative information is different and an old one. Broached in the 1898 issue of the *Journal of the American Statistical Association,* the matter has been debated episodically and heatedly since then. Part of the debate, perhaps most of it, is gratuitous, since no good study exploits only one kind of information, though either qualitative or quantitative may be implicit in a study that stresses its counterparts (Boruch, 1976; Boruch and Wortman, 1979). It is gratuitous also in being the result of qualitative researchers who are dismally ignorant of quantitative methods and quantitatively trained researchers with an equally parochial view. Neither side seems aware of frequently occurring forms of each approach. For instance, the union is evidenced—at least in limited ways, numbers, prose, and pictures—by annual reports, such as the *Condition of Education,* that bear no policy (Wohlstetter and Boruch, 1980). It is exploited in other ways, notably using case and ethnographic approaches in randomized tests (Chavez et al., 1981). Still, understanding the union—when it is useful and when it is not, how to achieve it economically and when to exploit it—is important and ought to be explored. And as McLaughlin (in Pincus, 1980) suggests, learning how to combine the information well is not easy. The explorations that have been done, so far, take the form of producing essays or publishing complaints. Each is a fine reminder about what we ought to be doing, but are not overwhelming in more than a few other respects.

It may seem presumptuous to argue that statisticians must learn about nonstatistical methods in order to better learn how to exploit their designs. But is is hard to see how good designs can be exploited better at the local, state, and national levels without that education.

CONCLUSION

What is the future of field experiments in planning and evaluating education programs? The answer lies partly in answers to other questions, especially about how the idea can be actualized in policy. That higher quality tests *should* be a matter for law and policy is fundamental in recommendations of the Holtzman Report.

Answers to "how" must be ecumenical, for what we can learn about field tests stems from a variety of disciplines. That spirit of intellectual exchange is rather less common than it should be. This is changing if we judge by products of SSRC and NAS efforts by Riecken et al. (1974) and Raizen and Rossi (1981). The answers must be egalitarian and be repeated, since the idea cannot be expected to prevail against transient and sometimes poorly informed public representatives. There is reason to be optimistic here, in small ways, judging from the participation of technically capable people on a few legislative committees at the state and federal levels.

The future also depends on how problems discussed here and ones omitted are solved. Old in principle and rather neglected, measuring and assuring integrity of treatment and of response, designing for utility, understanding the capability of those responsible for execution, and so on can be very difficult. The occurrence of the problems in agricultural and physical experiments may be less frequent than in the social sector, but they have indeed occurred. Expanding the idea of obtaining decent evidence on relative effects of social programs, at least occasionally, affords the opportunity to invent durable clusters of managerial, legislative, institutional, *and* technical approaches to their resolution.

The future depends too on repeatedly addressing basic questions that reappear over time and level of governance. The need to decide what questions should be asked in evaluation, and when experiments are appropriate and when they are not, is both persistent and critical. Each decision requires time for negotiation among principals. Each depends on whether there is any willingness and ability to use results, as in any applied research. Each depends on level of governance, since there is no guarantee that questions of interest at the federal level, for example, will be of any interest at all to local school districts. None of this is easy to gauge before the results appear, but the recent systematic efforts by evaluators to anticipate those factors is promising. The process is complicated further because there are many ways to obtain evidence. Some may be as good or better than controlled field tests, and this requires some effort to map conditions under which clinical cases or structural models will suffice.

Despite a statistical candor in the United States that is unmatched by any developed country and despite increased attention to quality of evidence in popular science writing, public interest in program effects is not especially uniform. What interest there is can be sustained, if not increased, through policy. Randomized field tests and other vehicles for better estimation are a small but important part of the latter. It can be enlarged only with vigorous participation of the community of researchers.

NOTES

1. A digest of all recommendations is given in Boruch et al. (1981). The full report, to be published as Boruch and Cordray (forthcoming), is available as a reproduced manuscript from the Office of the Assistant Secretary for Management, U.S. Department of Education, Washington, D.C. and from the Educational Resources Information Center (ERIC, ED192466). A parallel report stemming from the 1978 Educational Amendments was issued in March 1981 by the National Academy of Sciences Committee on Program Evaluation (Raizen and Rossi, 1981). Two other independent reports are pertinent. The first was developed by Pincus and his colleagues (1980), based on Rand Corporation research. The second, produced by Cronbach and

others (1980), is based on work by Stanford University's Consortium for Evaluation Research.

2. Analogous problems, of course, occur in popular and scientific reporting about statistics as well. See Kruskal and Mosteller (1979), for instance, on ways in which the phrase "representing sampling" is used in scientific and nonscientific literature.

REFERENCES

BORUCH, R. F. (1976) "On Common contentions about randomized experiments" pp. 158-194 in G. V. Glass (ed.) Evaluation Studies Review Annual, 3. Beverly Hills: Sage.

——— (1975) "Coupling randomized experiments and approximations to experiments." Sociological Methods and Research 4: 31-53.

——— and D. S. CORDRAY [eds] (forthcoming) An Appraisal of Educational Program Evaluations: Federal, State, and Local Agencies. New York: Cambridge

BORUCH, R. F. and H. GOMEZ (1979) "Sensitivity, bias, and theory in impact evaluations," pp. 139-170 in L. Datta and R. Perloff (eds.) Improving Evaluations. Beverly Hills: Sage.

BORUCH, R. F. and P. M. WORTMAN (1979) "Implications of educational evaluation for evaluation policy," pp. 309-361 in D. Berliner (ed.) Review of Research in Education, Volume 7. Washington, DC: American Educational Research Association.

BORUCH, R. F., A. J. McSWEENY, and E. J. SODERSTROM (1978) "Bibliography: illustrative randomized field experiments." Evaluation Quarterly 4: 655-696.

BORUCH, R. F., D. S. CORDRAY, G. PION, and L. LEVITON (1981) "A mandated appraisal of evaluation practices" Educational Researcher 10: 10-13, 31.

BOX, J. F. (1981) "Gosset, Fisher, and the t distribution." American Statistician 25: 61-66.

BREGER, M. (forthcoming) "Social experiments and the law," in J. Ross et al (eds.) Ethical and Legal Problems in Social Research. New York: Academic Press.

BUNDA, M. A. (1981) "Some comments on the recommendations in the Holtzman project." Educational Researcher 10: 14.

CAMPBELL, D. T. and R. F. BORUCH (1975) "Making the case for randomized assignment to treatments by considering the alternatives: six ways in which quasi-experimental evaluations in compensatory education tend to underestimate effects," pp. 195-296 in C. A. Bennett and A. A. Lumsdaine (eds.) Central Issues in Social Program Evaluation. New York: Academic.

CHAVEZ, R. et al. (1981) An Evaluation of the Head Start Bilingual Bicultural Curriculum Development Project. Los Angeles: Juarez and Associates, Inc.

COCHRAN, W. B. (1976) "Early developments in comparative experimentation," pp. 1-27 in D. B. Owen (ed.) On the History of Probability and Statistics. Basel: Marcel Dekker.

CONNER, R. F. (1977) "Selecting a control group: an analysis of the randomization process in twelve social reform programs." Evaluation Quarterly, 1, 2: 195-244.

COOK, T. D. and D. T. CAMPBELL [eds.] (1979) Quasi-Experimentation: Design and Analysis Issues in Field Settings. Chicago: Rand McNally.

CORSI, J. R. and T. L. HURLEY (1979) "Pilot study report on the use of the telephone in administrative fair hearings." Administrative Law Review 31, 4: 484-524.

CRONBACH, L. J. and Associates (1980) Toward Reform of Program Evaluation. San Francisco: Jossey-Bass.

DATTA, L. (1979) "Better luck this time: from federal legislation to practice in evaluating vocational education," pp. 37-78 in T. Abramson, C. K. Tittle, and L. Cohen (eds.) Handbook of Vocational Education Evaluation. Beverly Hills: Sage.

DAVIS, D. (1980) "Standardized evaluation of education programs." Presented at the Israel-U.S. Seminar on Evaluation Research, Ministry of Culture and Education, Hebrew University of Jerusalem, Israel, June.

DICKINSON, K. P. and R. W. WEST (1981) The Impacts of Counseling and Education Subsidy Programs. Menlo Park, CA: SRI International.

GILBERT, J. P., R. J. LIGHT, and F. MOSTELLER (1977) "Assessing social innovations: an empirical bases for policy," pp. 185-242 in W. B. Fairley and F. Mosteller (eds.) Statistics and Public Policy. Reading, MA: Addison-Wesley.

HENDRICKS, M. (forthcoming) "Service delivery assessment: qualitative evaluation at the cabinet level," in N. L. Smith (ed.) New Directions for Program Evaluation: Federal Efforts to Develop New Evaluation Methods. San Francisco: Jossey-Bass.

HOUSE, E. (1980) "Reactions to the Holtzman report." presented at the annual meeting of the Evaluation Research Society, Washington, D.C.

KRUSKAL, W. and F. MOSTELLER (1979) "Representative sampling, I: Non-scientific prose." International Statistical Review 47: 13-24.

LYONS, C. et al. (1978) Evaluation and School Districts. Los Angeles: Center for the Study of Evaluation.

MOSTELLER, F., S. P. GILBERT, and B. McPEEK (1980) "Reporting standards and research strategies: agenda for the editor." controlled Clinical Trials 1, 1: 37-58.

PILLEMER, D. B. and R. J. LIGHT (1979) "Using the results of randomized experiments to construct social programs: three caveats," pp. 717-726 in L. Sechrest et al. (eds.) Evaluation Studies Review Annual, Volume 4. Beverly Hills: Sage.

PINCUS, J. et al. (1980) Educational evaluation in the public policy setting (R-2502-RC). Santa Monica: Rand Corporation.

RABINOVITCH, N. L. (1973) Probability and Statistical Inference in Ancient and Medieval Jewish Literature. Toronto: University of Toronto Press.

RAIZEN, S. and P. ROSSI [eds.] (1981) Program Evaluation in Education: When? How? To What Ends? Washington, DC: National Academy of Sciences.

RE, E. D. and others (1981) Experimentation in the Law: Report of the Federal Judicial Center Advisory Committee on Experimentation in the Law. Washington, DC: FJC.

RICKEL, A. V. et al. (1979) "Description and evaluation of a preventive mental health program for preschoolers." Journal of Abnormal Child Psychology, 7: 101-112.

RIECKEN, H. W. et al. (1974) Social Experimentation. New York: Academic.

RIVLIN, A. M. (1971) Systematic Thinking for Social Action. Washington, DC: Brookings Institution.

ROBINS, P. K. and R. W. WEST (1981) Labor Supply Response to the Seattle and Denver Income Maintenance Experiments. Menlo Park, CA: SRI International.

ROSSI, P. H., R. A. BERK, and K. J. LENIHAN (1980) Money, Work, and Crime: Experimental Evidence. New York: Academic.

SECHREST L. and R. REDNER (1979) Strength and integrity of Treatments in Evaluation Studies. Washington, DC: National Criminal Justice Reference Service, National Institute of Law Enforcement and Criminal Justice, Law Enforcement Assistance Administration, U.S. Department of Justice.

SPENCER, B. D. (1980) Benefit-Cost Analysis of Data Used to Allocate Funds. New York: Springer Verlag.

TROCHIM, W. and C. SPIEGELMAN (1981) "The relative assignment variable approach to selection bias in pretest/posttest group designs," pp. 376-381 in Proceedings of the Survey Research Methods Section, American Statistical Association, 1980. Washington, DC: ASA.

U.S. General Accounting Office (1978) Assessing Social Program Impact Evaluations: A Checklist Approach. Washington, D.C.: Author, Program Analysis Division and the Institute for Program Evaluation (PAD-79-2).

WOHLSTETTER, P. and R. F. BORUCH (1980) "Numbers, prose and pictures: a review of the 'Condition of Education.' " Proceedings of the National Academy of Education. Washington, DC: NAE.

ZWEIG, F. M. and K. E. MARVIN [eds.] (1981) Educating Policy-Makers for Evaluation: Legislation. Beverly Hills: Sage.

4

Mary M. Kennedy
The Huron Institute

THE ROLE OF EXPERIMENTS IN
IMPROVING EDUCATION

Ever since Campbell and Stanley (1963) wrote their treatise on experimental and quasi-experimental research designs, evaluators have advocated the use of true experiments, with randomized assignment of units to program alternatives, as a valuable source of evidence for selecting program alternatives. From the evaluator's point of view, true experiments are preferable since they make the job of inferring program effects much easier. But since inferential power may be difficult to explain to program administrators, many evaluators promote the use of true experiments by arguing their programmatic advantages. Mosteller (1981) and Gilbert et al. (1975), for example, have pointed out the value of experimentation in the testing of innovations by demonstrating the frequency with which innovations turn out *not* to be as effective as anticipated. Boruch and Cordray (1980) have pointed to their value in planning, and suggest that new programs, program variations, or program components could be experimentally tested before being implemented on a larger scale. The Social Science Research Council (1974) advocated the use of experimental techniques for a variety of different purposes, and Gilbert and Mosteller (1972) argue that without experimentation, im-

AUTHOR'S NOTE: The research described in this chapter was supported jointly by the National Institute of Education and the Office of Evaluation and Management, U.S. Education Department. The opinions expressed here, however, are solely those of the author.

provements come only through a slow and wasteful process of natural selection.

Knowing that program administrators may be reluctant to implement one of the most critical features of experiments—random assignment—these authors have also defended the use of experiments against a myriad of counterarguments. For example, with regard to the ethical problems associated with random assignment, Gilbert et al. (1975) point out that there are also ethical problems associated with haphazardly implementing and changing programs without knowledge of their lasting benefits; and Campbell (1975) suggests comparing different treatment variations, rather than comparing treated groups with nontreated groups, so that no client goes unserved. With regard to the feasibility of conducting experiments, Boruch (1975) and Rezmovic, Cook, and Dobson (1981) offer a variety of practical strategies for implementing true experiments. Finally, Campbell (1972) recognized that a major counterinfluence to experiments was often the program directors' commitment to their program, and suggests that program directors modify their posture from one of advocating programs to one of advocating careful investigation of social problems.

Despite the continued enthusiasm of researchers and evaluators for these strategies, randomized experimental comparisons of alternative courses of action continue to be a small minority of the evaluations that are conducted, thus suggesting either that these arguments have not reached the right audiences, or that there may be other reasons for not conducting field experiments—reasons that have not yet been addressed. This chapter will present evidence suggesting that, where school districts are concerned, the latter may be the case, and that the problems associated with experiments are not inherent in the experiments themselves, but rather in the organizational context in which field experiments must be set.

The evidence comes from a study currently being conducted by The Huron Institute (Kennedy et al., 1980). During the course of this study, project staff visited 25 school districts to determine how evaluations and test data were used and what appeared to influence use. These districts ranged in size from 4000 students to over 200,000 students, and were situated in 14 states across the country.

During the course of these interviews, literally thousands of references were made to a wide range of empirical data which had been used—tests, studies, management information systems, surveys, and other kinds of research and evaluation information—but only three planned field experiments. By field experiment, we do not mean the broad class of summative evaluations that are frequently conducted, and which use statistically contrived or normative estimates of a "no treatment" condition; rather, we mean a narrower class of studies that were designed a priori to compare the relative benefits of two or more alternatives. Out of over 400 interviews, we found exactly three such studies being used. After describing these three examples, we will discuss some of the reasons why more were not used.

THREE EXAMPLES OF COMPARATIVE FIELD EXPERIMENTS

One district initiated a pilot after-school Title I program, and evaluated the after-school relative to the school day version of Title I. The study was fairly thorough. Not only were tests scores compared, but parents and school staff involved in the program were interviewed, and logistical arrangements regarding student transportation were investigated. The first findings to be released included everything but the outcome data—that is, the first findings related to implementation and to attitudes about the after-school program. These early findings were so positive that the district decided to convert its entire Title I program to an after-school program without waiting to see the outcome data. As it turned out, the latter data supported the decision, so it was not possible to ascertain whether the decision would have been reversed had the data not supported the decision.

The other two examples both occurred in one district. One study consisted of contrasts between classrooms with aides and those without, and the evaluators concluded that aides were costly and had little or no value in terms of children's academic achievement. The school board did not respond by eliminating all aides, however. Instead, it decided that those programs already employing aides could continue to do so, but that any new program proposals that included aides would be closely scrutinized. The second study addressed the question of whether categorical programs were more effective when children received their extra services within the class or when they were pulled out of class. The evaluators compared three alternatives: in-class, pull-out, and "principal's choice." The data suggested that in-class alternative were superior. These findings were considered in conjunction with other data which indicated that several children were being pulled from their regular classes for more than one program, and were, as a result of these moves, actually spending less time in instruction than were children in only one categorical program. The administration developed a policy limiting each child to one categorical program; it did not rule out the use of pull-out programs.

These three studies were not the only *comparisons* made, but they were the only comparisons that were based on planned field experiments. There were dozens of examples in which people analyzed patterns in extant test data, observed different buildings, or otherwise engaged in exploratory comparisons. In addition, there were several examples of summative evaluations, in which the "comparison" group was statistically contrived. These three studies are unique, however, in that they compared real alternatives and were designed in advance to do so.

Why Only Three?

There are probably dozens of reasons why more such studies had not been conducted and used, but the data suggest that the most salient reasons were not related to problems associated with conducting field experiments, but rather with the inherent characteristics of the districts themselves. Although the interviews were designed to learn how people used evaluation and test information, they were structured to first learn what issues interviewees were facing, and then to learn whether or how empirical information was used to address those issues. Many of the issues people discussed were quite complex, and interviewees were encouraged to discuss the history of the issue, how it arose, what considerations were involved in trying to solve a problem, what data had been or would be used, and so on. These discussions suggested that four reasons for experimental inactivity were particularly strong.

The Issues Themselves. Although the interviews were designed in such a way that each interviewee could, in principle, at least, discuss a unique issue, in fact certain issues arose repeatedly. These issues provide a first clue about why field experiments are not done more often: most of the questions people pose are not answerable by experimentation. That is, they are not questions about the relative benefits of alternative courses of action. Here are the most frequently discussed issues.

Among policy makers, that is, school board members, superintendents, and senior administrators, the primary issues raised were these:

- How to comply with various federal requirements;
- How to reduce costs in the face of declining enrollment;
- What to do about student behavior problems such as absenteeism, vandalism, and drug abuse; and
- What kind of testing policies and programs the district should have.

Among program directors and curriculum coordinators, that is, the middle management in the districts, the issues were these:

- How to meet programmatic responsibilities without having supervisory authority;
- How to make sure the program complies with regulations;
- How to maintain or increase funding; and
- How to improve the program.

Among building principles, the primary issues were these:

- How to implement district policies;
- How to manage the building—this includes not only student instruction, but also student behavior and teacher morale;
- How to improve programs in the building.

Finally, among teachers, the issues included:

- How to meet students' instructional needs;
- How to meet students' social and emotional needs; and
- How to know whether a child should be referred to, or belongs in, a special program.

These issues have been purposefully phrased here as "how-to" questions, even though interviewees rarely presented them in such explicit terms. But even phrased this way, the intent of the questions was rarely one of "which alternative should I pursue" as much as it was "I know what I want to have happen, but how do I get the system to budge?" Take, for example, a program director who wants to improve a program. The director may know that the program is not being implemented in half the school buildings. But may also know the following:

- Teachers avoid using materials because they don't know how.
- There is no money to support staff training.
- Even if there were money, the union contract restricts the amount of time teachers can spend on inservice training.
- Even if there were money and no time constraints, the program director may not have the authority to impose such training—that decision would have to be made by building principals or the superintendent.

For this hypothetical director, then, the issue is not one of which alternative, but rather how to get *any* alternative implemented.

Extant Constraints. But that is not the only reason why comparative field experiments are so rarely done. Sometimes the question of how to do something translates into how to design a program or a policy that can be accommodated by the existing system. Take the issue of student behavioral problems. Several districts were grappling with policies about drug abuse, student absences, or vandalism. School boards ultimately had to develop these policies, although superintendents and senior administrators often developed draft policies, recommendations, or position papers. Such practices are common when issues are broad or complex. As an example, this issue included such subissues as: to what extent should building principals have autonomy in their discipline strategies; should the district sanction corporal punishment; under what circumstances should police be brought in; what rights do students have; and how can due process procedures be established for students?

Now, in principle at least, a reasonably large school district could develop a series of alternative discipline policies, randomly assign school buildings to policies, and engage in a systematic comparison of policies, to determine which has the greatest ultimate effect on student behavior. Such a study would present some fascinating methodological problems to researchers, but it could be done and it could be very informative.

However, it may not be feasible, since each of the alternative policies under consideration would have to:

- Comply with all legislated or litigated rights of students;
- Be approved by the local police department as being consistent with the criminal laws;

- Be approved by the company that insures school buildings;
- Be approved by the teachers union;
- Be approved by the principle's association; and
- Be approved by parents or the community as a whole.

That is a lot of constraints. And the space that intersects these six sets of concerns may not be very large. Furthermore, even though more than one option may exist in that space, most policy makers will be exhausted by the time they find even one option within it, and will not be anxious to find others. The first solution they find will become the policy. Hence, no comparative field experiment will be conducted.

Multiple Criteria Involved in Selection. A third reason for the lack of field experiments is that even when the problem is posed as one of selecting among alternatives, field experiments may not be appropriate tools for making the decision. An example of such a choice can be derived from a common problem facing school districts today: declining enrollment. If enrollment has declined to the point where fewer buildings are needed, the notion of randomly selecting buildings to close, or of studying the effects of alternate closure plans simply did not arise. Buildings were selected for closure or for conversion to another purpose by considerations such as these:

- Which building's enrollment has declined the most;
- Which buildings have another school nearby that the remaining children can attend;
- Which combinations of closures allow students to be reallocated without leading segregation, or without leaving the district with too few buildings accessible to the handicapped;
- What the heating and maintenance costs are of different buildings;
- What the busing costs will be of alternative closures;
- Which neighborhoods have already lost schools recently;
- Which neighborhoods are growing.

Students' achievement, or the quality of programs in schools, is rarely a criterion, although one district's research department had conducted some ad hoc comparisons of test scores in small schools versus large ones to see if the size of the building appeared to have an effect on scores. (It did not.)

Furthermore, in addition to the selection criteria listed above, plans for closures must be approved of by the community, and that approval is extremely hard to obtain. Parents often buy homes in order to send their children to particular neighborhood schools, and property values are affected by the presence of schools in the neighborhood. Considerations such as these prevent districts from even considering the possibility of experimentally testing alternative closure plans.

Problems of Deleting Programs. There is yet a fourth reason for so few experiments. Consider the outcome of one of the experiments that was conducted: the study showing the lack of benefit from teacher aides did not lead to a deletion of aides from all programs—rather, *new* programs which proposed to use aides were to be scrutinized. Comparisons of any kind rarely lead administrators to stop a program. Our interviewees' references to studies other than planned experiments also demonstrate this problem. In one district, for instance, an ex post facto comparison of the effects of a computer-assisted math program suggested that the computers were very expensive and that children did essentially no better or worse for having participated in the program. The board did not drop the program, but instead decided not to expand it. In another district, a "back-to-basics" program was established at the request of the community. The program is considered to be a pilot program, and is currently being evaluated. But several interviewees there indicated that the program would have to do substantial damage to children before it would be cancelled, because parents wanted it. In this case, constituent demand was a more important criterion than was program quality.

Problems associated with deleting programs stem from more than the fact that they have constituents. Programs have histories. They consist of physical space, materials, staff, students, and organizational arrangements that put all these things together. Once they are established, even those programs without strong constituent support are hard to stop because the act of stopping entails a number of other difficult decisions. There may be due process considerations associated with laying off or transferring staff to other programs; there are materials to be stored, sold, or converted to another purpose, there are students who need to be assigned to other programs, and the physical space must be divided among other competing programs. The complexities involved on the management side of change alone can be overwhelming. Indeed, these problems have led some of the districts we visited to stop applying for federal funds to *start* new programs, because they knew they could not afford to continue them once the funds ran out, and they knew they would not be able to discontinue them.

These four obstacles to experimentation may be more difficult to overcome than the concerns about ethics and feasibility of planned experiments that are frequently discussed in the literature. There is a common theme running through all these points, and it has to do with the characteristics of complex systems such as school district bureaucracies. The first point, for example, emphasizing the difficulty of getting the system to budge, highlights the system inertia that is encountered by an individual or group within the system that wants to move toward a particular goal. The problem of getting something done is faced by every principal, program director, or policy maker—anyone whose goal is to modify the behaviors of others—but the problem is particularly salient for program directors since they tend not to control the incentives that could be used to motivate teachers or principals.

The second point, regarding the variety of constraints that must be accommodated in designing a new course of action, also indicates a system problem, in that new strategies cannot be based only on a determination of which course would be best for beneficiaries, but instead must be developed to fit within a number of existing system characteristics. And several constraints imposed on potential new developments are themselves intractable.

The third point, on the variety of criteria that have to be considered for a decision such as selecting schools to close, demonstrates the different and sometimes competing criteria that need to be considered in making a selection. That schools are being closed today suggests that changes can be made, but the multiple interest groups who become involved in the decisions, the high emotion that is often displayed during these deliberations, and the length of time taken to reach these decisions all point to the difficulty of initiating such a change.

Finally, the fourth point, regarding the difficulty of stopping a program alternative once it has begun, also suggests that system complexity is a major obstacle to progress in bureaucracies, so much so that some of our interviewees were reluctant to start new alternatives that they might not be able to stop. Presumably, the problems in stopping a course of action once it has begun are analogous to those of starting a course of action: accommodating the several system constraints, modifying incentives, meeting the concerns of a variety of interest groups, and orchestrating the myriad of management details associated with the decision.

CONCLUSION

School districts are organized systems—they contain many people working toward both individual and organizational goals; they entail divisions of labor and the concomitant need to synchronize the different divisions into the whole; they are influenced by their own organizational histories as well as by a variety of written and unwritten expectations that others have of them; and the people within them spend a considerable amount of their energy trying to get the systems better organized, in the hope that these organizational improvements will ultimately improve education. Indeed, even the three experiments that were located during the course of this investigation compared organizational alternatives rather than curriculum or instructional alternatives.

These findings suggest a rather limited role for experimentation in school districts. Advocates of true experiments base their arguments on the premise that the question of primary interest is one about the relative benefits to clients of different program alternatives. If that were true, then indeed true experiments would make a valuable contribution to decision-making. But the questions uppermost in the minds of our interviewees were only rarely about the effects of their actions or beneficiaries; instead, their predominant problems had to do either with the effects of their actions on the organization or with the effects of the organization on their potential for action.

These concerns for organizational process should not be taken to mean that there is no concern about the effectiveness of current procedures and practices. Indeed, most interviewees were quite aware of the test scores of children for whom they were responsible, and would, during the course of their conversations, explain that scores were higher or lower for certain groups, grade levels, or subject matters. This knowledge often appeared to be second nature to them and to be a normal part of their deliberations about changes. But the findings do suggest that when changes are being considered, the relative effectiveness of each alternative constitutes only one part of a wide range of issues that must be considered before one is selected.

Furthermore, issues other than effectiveness of options can pose such challenging problems that it is hard to muster up either the time or the energy to create and implement more than one alternative in order to learn which is really more effective. Instead of an experiment to compare alternatives, the usual strategy is to select the most feasible alternative, and then quickly turn one's attention to the more challenging problems of how to get the system to budge.

REFERENCES

BORUCH, R. F. (1975) "On common contentions about randomized field experiments," in R. F. Boruch and H. W. Reicken (eds.) Experimental Testing of Public Policy. Boulder, CO: Westview Press.

——— and D. CORDRAY (1980) An Appraisal of Educational Program Evaluations: Federal, State and Local Agencies. Evanston, IL: Northwestern University.

CAMPBELL, D. T. (1975) "A discussion on identifying alternative treatment programs," in R. F. Boruch and H. W. Reicken (eds.) Experimental Testing of Public Policy. Boulder, CO: Westview Press.

——— (1972) "Reforms as experiments," in C. H. Weiss (ed.) Evaluating Action Programs: Reading in Social Action and Education. Boston: Allyn & Bacon.

——— and J. C. STANLEY (1963) Experimental and Quasi-Experimental Designs for Research. Chicago: Rand McNally.

GILBERT, J. P. and F. MOSTELLER (1972) "The urgent need for experimentation," in F. Mosteller and D. Moynihan (eds.) On Equality of Education Opportunity. New York: Random House.

GILBERT, J. P., R. J. LIGHT, and F. MOSTELLER (1975) "Assessing social innovations: an empirical base for policy," in C. A. Bennett and A. A. Lumsdaine (eds.) Evaluation and Experiment. New York: Academic Press.

KENNEDY, M., R. APLING, and W. NEUMANN (1980) The Role of Evaluation and Test Information in Public Schools. Cambridge, MA: The Huron Institute

MOSTELLER, F. (1981) "Innovation and evaluation." Science 211: 881-886.

REZMOVIC, E. L., T. J. COOK, and L. D. DOBSON (1980) "Beyond random assignment: factors affecting evaluation integrity." Evaluation Review 5: 51-67.

Social Science Research Council (1974) "The purposes of social experimentation." Educational Researcher 3, 11: 5-10.

5

Jerome Johnston
Institute for Social Research
The University of Michigan

EVALUATION OF
CURRICULUM INNOVATIONS:
A Product Validation Approach

During the 1970s a number of cross-disciplinary themes appeared in the literature which taken together suggest a new paradigm for curriculum evaluation. In education there were several themes related to understanding the process of curricular innovation. Among these are the difficulties of implementing curricular innovations (Fullan and Pomfret, 1977), the resistance of teachers to innovating (House, 1974), and the importance of measuring implementation of innovations (Hall and Loucks, 1976). This last theme appeared in the literature on educational evaluation as well, with the emphasis on measuring implementation as part of a comprehensive evaluation study (Charters and Jones, 1973; Williams and Elmore, 1976; Leinhardt, 1977, 1980).

In medicine during the 1970s there was continued interest in a long–standing concern for measuring the effectiveness of medical innovations under ideal conditions ("efficacy"), and the problem of securing adherence to new treatment regimens when testing new drugs (OTA, 1978). In other fields, such as criminal justice, concern with implementation emerged late in the decade. Typical of the concern is a

AUTHOR'S NOTE: The research was carried out under a contract with the National Institute of Education (NIE-400-76-0096). Special thanks are due to Terrence Davidson, Paul Wortman, Bob Wise, Ralph Straton, and Gaea Leinhardt for critiques of various drafts of this chapter.

review article on "strength and integrity of treatments" by Sechrest and Redner (1979). These authors make the case that innovations in the field of criminal justice have been shown to be ineffective for the most part, but that in the evaluation studies that reached this conclusion the innovations were implemented at such low levels their true potential was probably never tested.

Together, these concerns suggest to the author a model for evaluating new curricular innovations which emphasizes assessment of the effectiveness of innovations under conditions of ideal use, assessing degree of implementation as part of the study, and incorporating the implementation information in analyses of the evaluation data. The approach is called a "product validation"; this chapter develops the logic for the approach and provides an example from a recent nationwide study assessing the effects of an instructional television package entitled *Freestyle*.

Implementation Assessment

In the early 1970s, Charters and Jones (1973) alerted the educational research community to the danger of "appraising non-events in program evaluation." Their own experience led them to surmise that many evaluation studies reporting little or no effects from the innovation being studied were in fact not assessing the innovation at all, because the innovation was so poorly implemented in the study. Shortly after this, Williams and Elmore (1976) devoted a whole book to social program implementation. Other authors in the evaluation field urged evaluators to pay closer attention to implementation or "process" evaluation (Patton, 1978).

Education has led most other fields in developing measures of implementation. Two separable strands appear in the literature: one emphasizing understanding the process of innovation adoption, the other emphasizing understanding the relationship between the innovation and student outcomes. Fullan and Pomfret (1977) provide a major review of the first strand. In their review they include three studies which used implementation data to explain student outcomes (Hess and Buckholdt, 1974; Leinhardt, 1974; Hall and Loucks, 1976). For example, Leinhardt found that "degree of implementation" accounted for 35 percent of the variance in achievement in a second grade program of adaptive education. But in the Fullan and Pomfret review of such findings are used only to validate the assessment of implementation, not to justify one curriculum innovation over another.

Project Follow Through has provided an opportunity for much of the research on the second strand—measuring implementation to understand student outcomes (Stallings, 1974; Kaskowitz and Stallings, 1975; Leinhardt, 1977). Each of these authors collected extensive information on the presence in each classroom of key elements of each Follow Through variation. Two articles by Leinhardt (1977, 1980) highlight the problems of data reduction of implementation information and the difficulties entailed in relating complex process information to "level of summative success." But they are important contributions to furthering the use of implementation data in evaluation studied.

Efficacy and Effectiveness

Two concepts from the medical field—efficacy and effectiveness—are useful in understanding the importance of proper implementation. Virtually everyone in society at some time or other needs a doctor to correct or prevent some physiological malfunction. When doctors choose a medicine or medical procedure to meet this need, they select an "approved" product or procedure. At one time it was only an innovation and the FDA or other agency required proof that it was efficacious before doctors could use it routinely with patients. The Office of Technology Assessment (1978: 16) defines efficacy and effectiveness in this way:

> *Efficacy:* the probability of benefit to individuals in a defined population from a medical technology applied for a given medical problem under ideal conditions of use.

> This report differentiates efficacy from effectiveness. Effectiveness is concerned with the benefit of a technology under average conditions of use. An effective technology has positive benefits for those people who are treated with the technology in a typical medical setting. Although the efficacy of a drug, for example, may be evaluated for individuals in a research setting, its effectiveness in an average setting may be influenced by variables [which] are more rigorously controlled in a research setting. Thus, the efficacy and the effectiveness of a drug may differ.

As potential patients, anxious for cures and fearful of dangerous side effects, we all laud the demand for both types of evidence. As parents and students we seem less concerned for similar evidence regarding educational products.

In education, the concept of efficacy is implicit in the creation of the National Diffusion Network with its certification of "effective" programs by the Joint Dissemination Review Panel. Fullan and Pomfret (1977) and House (1974) are critical of this "certified innovation" approach, largely because of their appreciation of problems of implementing innovations. However, the notion of certified innovation is at the heart of a "product validation" approach. We will return to these criticisms at the end of this chapter, and see if a blending of the two approaches to curriculum reform is possible.

"Routinization of Innovations": Implications for Evaluation

Curriculum innovations vary from prepackaged products requiring simple insertion into existing instructional processes to complex organizational changes requiring a restructuring of the classroom and of teacher behaviors. But, no matter how little change an innovation demands, Fullan and Pomfret (1977: 391) conclude, as have others, that "effective implementation...requires time, personal interaction and contacts, in-service training, and other forms of people-based support...if the difficult process of unlearning old roles and learning new ones is to occur. Equally clear is the absence of such opportunities on a regular basis during the planning and implementation of most innovations."

Taking this finding into account, Hall (et al., 1975: 56) speculates, "one of the key reasons, we think, that so many 'evaluation' reports conclude with no significant differences between experimental innovative efforts and comparison efforts is [that] data are collected during the first cycle of use of the innovation when most of the users are...not yet using the innovation effectively. Thus, it is unreasonable to anticipate significant achievement gains." Hall and others in the field of innovation dissemination make the general point that adoption of any new innovation is an extended *process* which is characterized by an adopter showing increasingly greater competence at producing the intended innovative behaviors with each successive use of the new program. Hall does not consider an innovation to be "adopted" until its key elements have been "routinized"—a process which takes time and repeated experience with the new product or program. For example, the Agency for Instructional Television creates instructional video series for classroom use. In general, each series fits into existing curricular goals and requires relatively little change by teachers or schools; yet they estimate that teachers do not use a new instructional series properly until their second or third year. Such a waiting period is impractical when it comes to assessing the value of a new product.

A more timely solution is to test a new product with adopters who have been specially trained to aproximate the kind of use expected after two to three years of normal dissemination, adoption, and adaptation. The author calls this approach a "product validation." This strategy was used to evaluate the efficacy of the *Freestyle* television series—a new product designed to reduce the limiting effects of sex-role stereotypes among 9-12 year olds (Johnston et al., 1980). The remainder of this chapter develops three topics. First description is presented of how the product validation was designed and executed. Second is how strength of the treatment was "modeled" and implementation assessed. Finally, data on implementation are related to change in the target population, providing evidence of the value of both the "product validation" design and implementation measurement.

THE *FREESTYLE* PRODUCT VALIDATION

Freestyle is an educational television series distributed on the Public Broadcasting Service (PBS). It premiered in the fall of 1978. The 13 half-hour segments of programming and supporting print materials (a teacher guide and student workbook) are designed to reduce sex-role stereotypes among 9 to 12 year olds. In providing over $4 million to create this series, the National Institute of Education hoped to provide a high quality intervention for the upper elementary grades in the area of career education. If successful, this series would lead children— especially girls and minorities—to choose career-related activities that are considered nontraditional for their sex and minority status. Later in life these childhood activities would articulate to nontraditional job choices.

The intervention is designed both for school and home use. Each of the half-hour dramas reaches a climax at the 15-minute point. For the school version the shows are broadcast in 15-minute modules, permitting students to view first a problem situation in sex-role behavior. In classroom discussion following this episode, a class generates its own solution to the problem. A day or two later the class views the Hollywood resolution of the problem. For home use, both quarter-hours are broadcast together as a single half-hour show.

This chapter focuses on testing the efficacy of *Freestyle* in a classroom setting using a "product validation" approach. In brief, this entails simulating, at the time the series was introduced, the type and intensity of use that might be anticipated with teachers who had used the series for two or three years.

The research design was a randomized experiment in which schools in a district were assigned to either an experimental validation group or a control group. Although all of the teachers were volunteers, they did not know when they volunteered whether they would be assigned to the experimental or control group. The design is shown schematically in Figure 5.1. A pretest was administered to all children in September of 1978, one week before *Freestyle* was introduced nationally. During the ensuing 3-1/2 months, the series was used intensively in the validating classrooms. In January of 1979 a posttest was administered to the same children. The schematic shows intermediate measurement during the time of the intervention; one such measure was a weekly assessment of implementation in each of the validating classrooms. This is described in greater detail below.

The most intensive condition—classroom viewing and discussion—was established in a total of five locations. In three of these—Long Beach, California; Milwaukee, Wisconsin; and Ann Arbor, Michigan—the intensive condition was compared to only a control group. In two more locations—Worcester, Massachusetts and North Kansas City, Missouri—the intensive condition was compared not only to a control condition, but also to another validation group that had experienced a less intensive regimen, that of mere viewing of the TV series. For our purposes here, the focus is on assessing the efficacy of only the most intensive condition.

The Validating Regimen

The validating regimen included several elements. In a one-day training session, *Freestyle* was introduced to participating teachers and

	Sept 78		Jan 79	Nov 79
Site Type 1: Intensive School Use	O_1	CLASSROOM VIEW & DISCUSS $O_a....O_n$	O_2	(O_3)
	O_1	SCHOOL CONTROL	O_2	(O_3)

Where O_1=pretest, O_2=post-test, O_3=post-post test (Ann Arbor only), and $O_a....O_n$=intermediate measures.

Figure 5.1 Schematic of the Research Design

time was spent practicing the recommended method of using each component of the intervention, including each of the following activities which were presented as essential components for regular participation in the experiment.

I. Weekly, for 13 weeks

   (a) "Prep" students for each of two quarter-hour shows using the "Preview Activity" in the School Guide or your own questions. Minimum 5 minutes.
   (b) View the two shows on two separate days
   (c) Conduct discussions after each show using questions under "Talk Topics" in the Guide
   (d) Use one "More to Come" activity in another curricular area
   (e) Make entries (you or students) in "Activity Log"

II. During the 13-week period use the *Freestyle* Magazine with students as appropriate.

For the most part these components were derived from the developers' statements of what were essential parts of the curriculum. However, in the *Freestyle* study the essential ingredients were derived by negotiating between two groups: the designers of the curriculum and the school administrators and teachers in the validating cities.

The word "negotiating" is used purposely. The designers of *Freestyle* invested several years creating the curriculum plan, the TV shows, teacher guide, student magazine, and teacher training program. It was in their interest to see that the products were used and tested under the most ideal conditions. From their perspective this would include training teachers for several days in effective use of television in the classroom followed by specific instruction in how to use *Freestyle*. Several follow-up "refresher" sessions would be appropriate as well. In addition the developers hoped that teachers would spend many hours per week on *Freestyle* over and above the regimen listed above. In contrast to this, teachers in most classrooms—even those who might volunteer to validate an interesting new product—are interested in minimizing the disruption to their existing routines and curricular priorities. To them, time spent on *Freestyle* is time *not* spent on something else. The needs of these teachers must be taken into account in validating a new curricular product, because they represent the environment in which the product must ultimately compete.

The evaluator who assesses a new product should do the negotiating, since it is the evaluator's task to persuade a district to cooperate with the research. It can be argued that the designers ought to be involved in this process as well since they represent the proponents of maximum use, and it is they who ought to hear district people say "this much and no more will work here." However, sites which volunteer might agree to a stronger "dose" of the new product than would be realistic in other districts. The evaluator can represent the more "typical" districts in arriving at a regimen to be tested. When the validation study is finished, it is the evaluator's evidence which must convince interested audiences that the regimen used in the validation is a prototype of what other adopters could reasonably implement if they choose to adopt this new product.

Establishing the Regimen

To argue persuasively that the regimen was followed by teachers in this study it is necessary to establish two points: (1) the agents of change—the teachers in the validating sites—understood what was expected of them and could indeed produce the type of instructional behaviors that were required; (2) they faithfully produced these instructional behaviors throughout the experiment. The first requirement was handled in two ways. First, a requirement for selecting a district to participate was that there be a history of instructional television use by its teachers, and that participating teachers show some evidence of having used television in their instruction. A second feature was the provision of in-service training for all participating teachers. Fortunately, the curriculum designers for *Freestyle* had developed for the project a teacher training package to accompany the series. They agreed to train the validating teachers in each of the sites.

Activity type	Was any class time spent on this activity?	If any class time was spent, please indicate:		
		Date(s)	Time started	Time ended
1-Introduction to the show	No [ ] Yes [ ]			
2-Viewing the show	No [ ] Yes [ ]			
3-Discussion after the show	No [ ] Yes [ ]			
4-Other classroom activities	No [ ] Yes [ ]			

Figure 5.2   Example of *Freestyle* Activity Log for "Partners" (first half)

A third factor helped to establish a consistent regimen. Participating teachers spent a full day in training: one half-day devoted to the proper use of *Freestyle* and the second half to research procedures such as questionnaire administration. An important piece of the training in the second half-day was a discussion of each step in the regimen coupled with training in the completion of a weekly log of time spent on each part of the regimen. An example of this log is shown in Figure 5.2. This log serves two purposes. One is the obvious one of assessing compliance for evaluative purposes; the other is that it provides a weekly reminder to the teacher of what is expected. To reinforce this initial training, the evaluator's local coordinator in each site contacted each teacher twice in the first six weeks of the experiment to remind them of the regimen and detect any problems that might interfere with adherence.

Measuring Treatment Fidelity

These factors all contributed to initiating a treatment of a particular strength. But fidelity to the plan over the 13-week intervention is another issue. The term "fidelity," is Fulland Pomfret's and refers to the curriculum users being faithful to the plan. (Sechrest and Redner [1979] prefer the term "treatment integrity" to indicate the same thing.) Fidelity in this study was measured using teacher self-reports of particular behaviors used each week. The self-reports consist of time spent on task as shown in Figure 5.2. A teacher completed two charts during each week of the experiment.

How valid were these reports? In order to secure the most accurate implementation data possible, teachers were instructed how to complete the activity log. This was coupled with an appeal to be honest with the researchers and numerous assurances were given that no data on individual classroom or school performance would be seen by anyone within the district.

To determine the success of the procedure, a special approach was made to 20 teachers in two of the sites. The site coordinators—chosen because they were known to teachers in the district—asked these teachers whether they felt they were being candid in the logs. The conclusion of these two coordinators was that at least these twenty teachers had been quite frank.

Another bit of evidence to support the validity of the logs are provided by the logs themselves. There were very few instances of idealized records. In almost every log there was at least occasional noncompliance, and this seemed to follow a haphazard (and thus believable) pattern. In terms of time spent on different activities, the activities that were expected to vary from time to time did. These were the introductory activities and the postviewing discussions.

Implementation Index

If the data are believable, what do they say in the aggregate about compliance? To answer this question parsimoniously, a single index was constructed for each classroom which summarized degree of implementation across the experiment. Before describing the algorithm by which this was derived, consider the regimen and how the activity logs reflect to it. Each week a teacher was to have the children view two interrelated 15-minute shows. There was a routine surrounding each of these shows that entailed preparing the audience, viewing, and then discussing what was seen. In addition to this twice-weekly ritual, the teacher was to choose a supplementary activity from the Guide which would develop the sex-role theme in a separate curricular area. The activity log was set up to encourage the teacher to make an entry after each show. Completion of the supplementary activity could be noted on the log for either of the week's two shows.

Calculating a series level implementation score entailed two steps. This is diagrammed in Figure 5.3. In the first step, an implementation score ranging from 0-4 was calculated for each of the 26 episodes. One point was assigned for completing each of the three activities: preview presentation, viewing itself, and postviewing discussion. An additional point was given for doing a supplementary activity. In a second step these 26 separate implementation scores were summed, allowing a theoretical maximum of 104 points. Perfect compliance, however, requires only 91 points, since only one supplementary activity was required for every two shows.

In Table 5.1 the implementation score has been divided into quintiles, and the activity levels are shown for each quintile group. The 59 classrooms with the heaviest implementation (scores of 81-104) saw virtually all of the 26 TV shows accompanied by an introductory and follow-up activity. Supplementary activities average 17.1 and this exceeded the number required by three. The next lowest implementation group, with scores ranging from 61-80, had roughly the same viewing and discussion behavior, but was much lower on supplementary activities. they averaged only 4.5 out of 13 requested.

These two groups of classrooms, labeled five and six in Table 5.1, were selected as having implemented about as perfectly as could be expected. For purposes of the evaluation report of *Freestyle's* effects, only classrooms in these two categories were used for analysis. They comprised 82 percent of the experimental classrooms. The remaining implementation groups were declared to be too low to include in the analyses of a so-called "validation study." Table 5.2 shows that the numbers of students lost in the analyses in any one site range from a low of 3 percent of the total analytic sample to a high of 17 percent.

Such high levels of treatment implementation demonstrate what can be done with careful cultivation of validating groups. But it must be noted that the intervention—the *Freestyle* program—was judged by the validating teachers to be a very attractive and valued product. Adherence to a tough regimen is certainly greatly enhanced by an attractive product. Perhaps the degree of implementation is itself an indirect measure of the quality of the product being validated.

It should be noted that implementation was checked with control teachers as well. A questionnaire at the end of the project asked whether any units of material had been included in the curriculum which were similar to *Freestyle*. The data resulted in eliminating one classroom from the control group.

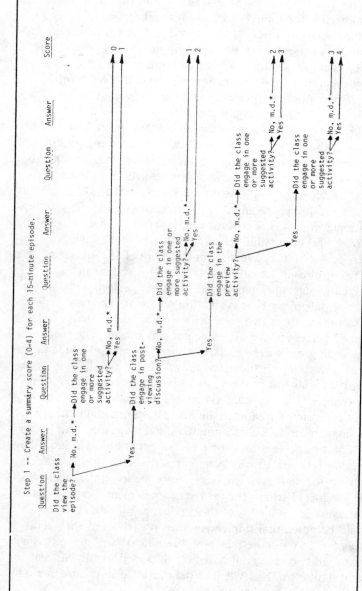

Step 1 -- Create a summary score (0-4) for each 15-minute episode.

Figure 5.3 Implementation Score Algorithm for Activity Log Data

*m.d. is used to designate records which were left blank or were otherwise ambiguous.

90

TABLE 5.1
Aggregate Mean Activity Levels for Different Implementation Groups
Intensive Classroom Use

Implementation Group[a]	No. of Classrooms	Mean Number of			
		Segments Seen	Segments Introduced	Segments Discussed	Supplementary Activities
Actual					
2 (0-20)	1	14.0	14.0	0.0	0.0
3 (21-40)	6	17.3	12.7	8.2	4.5
4 (41-60)	18	22.3	12.9	14.3	4.8
5 (61-80)*	57	24.5	22.2	22.8	4.5
6 (81-104)*	59	25.4	24.9	25.0	17.1
Average		24.2	21.7	21.8	9.7
n	141	141	141	141	141
Ideal		26	26	26	13

a For both school full and school view only, group 1 is the control group which had no *Freestyle* at all. In parenthesis after each group is the range of Implementation Scores contained in the group.

* The analyses for the product validation study were based on children in these classrooms only.

91

TABLE 5.2
Number of Students by Sites and Implementation Level

Implementation Group	Long Beach	Milwaukee	Worcester	Ann Arbor	North Kansas City
Control	429/35%	313/23%	283/31%	112/19%	—
2-3 (0-40)	—	27/02	128/14	—	—
4 (41-60)	107/09	134/10	23/03	100/17	48/13
5 (61-80)	291/24	516/37	249/28	150/26	135/37
6 (81-104)	395/32	390/28	217/24	227/38	185/50
	1222/100%	1380/100%	900/100%	589/100%	368/100%

The Effects of Underimplementation

The decision to retain only implementation groups five and six was based initially on political considerations. In the absence of time to examine whether there were real outcome differences between these two groups and those classrooms with lower implementation, it seemed most defensible to say that the evaluation results were based on data from only those classrooms that most critics could agree implemented *Freestyle* at a very high level. But how different were the results for students from classrooms in implementation groups 2-4? To investigate this, the effects for each level of implementation were charted for two outcome measures which showed very large changes for heavy users of *Freestyle:* attitude toward girls participating in athletics (football and basketball), and attitude toward girls doing mechanical activities (fixing a faucet, a bicycle, working on a car motor, and so on). The results are shown in Table 5.3 for four of the validating cities.

The data are taken from an analysis of covariance in which the posttest scores were regressed on the pretest. Adjusted posttest means are shown for each implementation level. (Individual level data are presented in the tables. The same pattern appears when classroom-level data are used.) Table 5.3 shows the data for attitude toward girls in athletics. The data are shown separately for boys and girls in each site because the pattern of results is somewhat different for the two groups. Rows one and two show the results in Long Beach. For boys, the adjusted posttest scores for the control group averaged 2.41, while those in classrooms at implementation levels five and six were a full one-half standard deviation higher, averaging 2.92 and 2.86 respectively. By contrast, those boys in classrooms with implementation level four had scores only 18 percent of a standard deviation above the control group scores. A similar picture appears for Long Beach girls, although the score for girls in level four classrooms is proportionally closer to the high implementing students than the control students.

The Long Beach data, then, lend support to the decision to exclude level four students from the analyses. Their small numbers would not have altered the original conclusion about efficacy of the intervention on this particular outcome measure because of the magnitude of effect in the high implementing classrooms and the larger proportion of high

TABLE 5.3
Adjusted Posttest Scores by Implementation Level: Attitude Toward Girls in Athletics
(1 = very bad idea; 4 = very good idea)

Sample	Signif[a]	Implementation Level					Total[b]
		Control	2-3	4	5	6	
1. Long Beach Boys	.00	2.41 (200)	—	2.58 (46)	2.92 (143)	2.86 (195)	2.70/.96 (584)
2. Long Beach Girls	.00	3.10 (174)	—	3.32 (43)	3.49 (126)	3.47 (160)	3.32/.72 (503)
3. Milwaukee Boys	.00	2.30 (115)	2.30 (8)	2.44 (62)	2.56 (239)	2.75 (155)	2.55/.95 (579)
4. Milwaukee Girls	.00	3.09 (141)	3.24 (16)	3.43 (58)	3.42 (228)	3.38 (180)	3.32/.70 (623)
5. Worcester Boys	NS	2.83 (130)	2.68 (53)	2.87 (12)	2.88 (118)	2.87 (114)	2.83/.91 (427)
6. Worcester Girls	.00	3.38 (131)	3.64 (72)	3.42 (10)	3.67 (124)	3.46 (93)	3.52/.67 (430)
7. Ann Arbor Boys	NS	2.85 (48)	—	3.09 (54)	3.07 (71)	3.06 (114)	3.03/.79 (287)
8. Ann Arbor Girls	NS	3.44 (59)	—	3.58 (42)	3.61 (66)	3.59 (103)	3.56/.49 (270)

Note: Adjusted mean scores from an analysis of covariance regressing the posttest scores on the pretest scores.

[a] Significance of the test of equal adjusted means in the analysis of covariance.

[b] The cell entries are the overall mean score, followed by the standard deviation.

implementing classrooms. With an outcome for which *Freestyle* had a more marginal effect it might have altered the conclusion.

Is the same pattern found in other sites? Among Milwaukee boys (row 3), the pattern is one of monotonically increasing effects with each higher level of implementation; but not for the girls (row 4). Here, the 58 girls in level four classrooms have the same posttest scores as those in higher implementing contexts. Among Worcester and Ann Arbor students there were no consistent effects of treatment for any levels of implementation, so the hypothesis cannot be tested. A similar pattern of results emerges from the data in Table 5.4. Students in classrooms with intermediate levels of implementation have appreciably lower scores than those in high implementing classrooms in four out of eight cases.

DISCUSSION

Overall, the data from *Freestyle* argue in favor of measuring and statistically controlling for implementation when it is important to avoid Type II error: saying that an intervention has no effect when indeed it does if it is properly implemented. In another curricular evaluation where treatment fidelity had not been so carefully nurtured, it would be all the more important to take implementation into account.

The evaluators' model of the *Freestyle* intervention was quite simplistic. Classroom discussion, which has a lot of important qualitative dimensions, was treated the same in every classroom. If at least ten minutes of discussion occurred it was coded as being present. With an intervention as carefully proscribed as this, and structured by weekly cues from the external environment (TV broadcasts), this model of the intervention is probably a reasonable representation for purposes of validating that the curriculum designers' recommended procedures had been followed. Implementation assessment with more complex interventions requiring organizational change would be much more difficult, but certainly worth trying given the potential of finding an innovation that does indeed work. (For assessment of more complex phenomena, see Fullan and Pomfret, 1977; Leithwood and Montgomery, 1980; Leinhardt, 1980; Johnston and Ettema, forthcoming.)

Observations on the length of time it takes for a product to be noticed, adopted, and adapted to the intricacies of local conditions

TABLE 5.4

Adjusted Posttest Scores by Implementation Level: Attitude Toward Girls in Mechanical Activities
(1 = very bad idea; 4 = very good idea)

Sample	Signif[a]	Implementation Level					Total[b]
		Control	2-3	4	5	6	
1. Long Beach Boys	.00	2.30 (199)	—	2.64 (46)	2.89 (144)	2.78 (196)	2.63/.89 (585)
2. Long Beach Girls	.00	2.68 (175)	—	3.05 (44)	3.08 (128)	3.16 (160)	2.96/.76 (507)
3. Milwaukee Boys	.00	2.36 (115)	2.44 (8)	2.33 (63)	2.57 (238)	2.66 (155)	2.53/.88 (579)
4. Milwaukee Girls	.00	2.74 (138)	3.25 (16)	3.04 (59)	2.98 (228)	3.03 (181)	2.96/.75 (622)
5. Worcester Boys	NS	2.47 (133)	2.47 (53)	2.72 (12)	2.64 (118)	2.72 (116)	2.60/.91 (432)
6. Worcester Girls	.00	2.86 (132)	3.22 (73)	3.09 (10)	3.41 (124)	3.23 (94)	3.17/.79 (433)
7. Ann Arbor Boys	.00	2.67 (49)	—	2.91 (54)	2.90 (73)	3.06 (115)	2.93/.75 (291)
8. Ann Arbor Girls	NS	3.27 (59)	—	3.33 (43)	3.30 (68)	3.37 (100)	3.32/.61 (270)

Note: Adjusted mean scores from an analysis of covariance regressing the posttest scores on the pretest scores.

[a] Significance of the test of equal adjusted means in the analysis of covariance.

[b] The cell entries are the overall mean score, followed by the standard deviation.

provide the impetus and justification for a special research paradigm in addition to simply measuring degree of implementation. This is the "product validation" design. As long as product potential and product delivery are confounded in a single study, it is unclear how to interpret the research results unless the data clearly support the innovation. This has rarely been the case with evaluation studies of the last ten years. If the data do not provide unqualified support for the new product, the question remains: is it the innovation or effective implementation that is at fault? If a product validation study concludes that a product has sufficient treatment strength to warrant further use, an additional study may be warranted which examines product effectiveness—impact under conditions more nearly approximating normal use. In this second study, the measurement of implementation would be even more important since the focus would be primarily on the process of delivery and how the process relates to outcomes that have already been normed (see Leinhardt, 1980). An analysis of implementation process would also uncover barriers in the delivery system that might stand in the way of achieving the treatment strength and integrity achieved in the validation study (Fullan and Pomfret, 1977; Leithwood and Montgomery, 1980). In the research on *Freestyle* this was handled by questionnaires to the validating teachers after they had finished the experiment and by interviews with administrators in the validating districts (see Johnston et al., 1980: 4-5).

Product Validation and Curriculum Reform

It was noted earlier that the "certified innovation" approach has its critics. Fullan and Pomfret (1977) as well as House (1974) argue that the "doctrine of transferability" which permeates federal strategies for change work against complete and effective implementation of educational innovations. There is merit in their argument, given what is known about the difficulty of securing implementation and the importance of "mutual adaptation" to make an innovation work properly in local settings. However, it appears to the author that two things are needed for effective curriculum reform: establishment of the efficacy of individual instructional innovations coupled with more investment in local efforts at adoption and adaptation. The latter should not occur on a large scale if the innovation has not been shown to be efficacious. The development of an innovation may require extensive experimentation with implementation, as urged by Fullan and Pomfret; but at some point each innovation that requires the investment of resources by school districts (new books, new technologies, organizational restructuring, or teacher retraining) should be shown to be efficacious enough to merit the investment. This position is based not on a political stance of how curriculum planning and reform should proceed, but rather on the pragmatic consideration that data on efficacy may be essential to secure the very kind of effective implementation the critics would like to see. Why are so few innovations implemented effectively? Berman and Pauly (1975) found that teachers perceive that they face difficult problems in trying to implement new innovations, including a lack of time and energy. House (1975) cites these and other reasons for underimplementation, including the absence of incentives for teachers to pay the price of innovating. His most telling criticism, however, is this: there is little indication that innovations are worth the effort!

What is meant by "worth the effort?" There are many aspects of an innovation which could lead teachers to value an innovation. Among these are the knowledge that struggling to implement it would result in one or more of the following:

(1) providing instruction in an area not met by existing material or activities but valued by the teacher or others in the district
(2) easing the task of instruction for the teacher
(3) motivating students (making them enthusiastic about participating in the learning experience)
(4) changing students in a way that was valued by the teacher and the system (higher achievement, more favorable attitudes, improved self-esteem, and so forth)

Of this list, only the first can result from a simple examination of materials; the remaining three are most easily obtained by information from a "product validation."

The notion of a "product validation" is not entirely unique, but it is clearly not a standard educational evaluation. Some time ago Scriven (1974) advocated that instructional designers provide both evidence of a need for a new product as well as evidence that a new product did any better than what it was to replace. Cronbach and his colleagues (1980) encourage a prototype testing before final installation of an innovation. Indeed, legislation in Texas and California requires that before new instructional products can be approved by the state, evidence must be provided that learners who use the materials will learn something as a result. Many of the educational labs do extensive testing of their products before large-scale dissemination. But it is not clear that what is required in any of these cases is the kind of efficacy test of the completed prototype which is implicit in the product validation model. It is clear that such a strategy is not a common feature of much of curricular development. Expense is clearly a factor; product validations are costly and perhaps not warranted for every new innovation. But the more costly the innovation and the greater the requirement for change in the adopting organization, the greater the need for such an approach.

REFERENCES

BERMAN, P. and E. PAULY (1975) Federal Programs Supporting Educational Change, Vol. II: Factors Affecting Change Agent Projects. Santa Monica, CA: Rand Corporation.

CHARTERS, W. W., Jr. and J. E. JONES (1973) "On the risk of appraising non-events in program evaluation." Educational Researcher 2, 11: 5-7.

CRONBACH, L. J., S. R. AMBRON, S. M. DORNBUSCH, R. D. HESS, R. C. HORNIK, D. C. PHILLIPS, D. F. WALKER, and S. S. WEINER (1980) Toward Reform of Program Evaluation. San Francisco: Jossey Bass.

FULLAN, M. and A. POMFRET (1977) "Research on curriculum and instruction implementation." Review of Educational Research 47, 2: 335-397.

HALL, G. E. and S. F. LOUCKS (1976) A Developmental Model for Determining Whether or Not the Treatment Really is Implemented. Research and Development Center for Teacher Education, University of Texas at Austin.

HALL, G. E., S. F. LOUCKS, W. L. RUTHERFORD, and B. W. NEWLOVE (1975) "Levels of use of the innovation: a framework for analyzing innovation adoption." Journal of Teacher Education 26, 1: 52-56.

HESS, R. and D. BUCKHOLDT (1971) "Degree of implementation as a critical variable in program evaluation." Presented at the meeting of the American Educational Research Association, Chicago, April.

HOUSE, E. (1974) The Politics of Educational Innovation. Berkeley, CA: McCutchan.

JOHNSTON, J. and J. ETTEMA (forthcoming) The Lessons of *Freestyle:* Creating Prosocial Television for Children. Beverly Hills: Sage.

——— and T. DAVIDSON (1980) An Evaluation of Freestyle. Ann Arbor: Institute for Social Research.

KASKOWITZ, D. and J. STALLINGS (1975) "An assessment of program implementation in project Follow Through." Presented at the annual meeting of the American Educational Research Association, Washington, D.C., April.

LEINHARDT, G. (1980) "Modeling and measuring educational treatment in evaluation." Review of Educational Research 50, 3: 393-420

——— (1977) "Program evaluation: an empirical study of individualized instruction." American Educational Research Journal 14, 3: 277-293.

——— (1974) "Evaluation of the implementation of a program of adaptive education at the second grade (1972-73)." Presented at the annual meeting of the American Educational Research Association, Chicago, April. (Appears, with minor revision, as "Evaluating an adaptive education program: Implementation to replication." Instructional Science 6 (1977): 223-257.)

LEITHWOOD, K. A. and D. J. MONTGOMERY (1980) "Evaluating program implementation." Evaluation Review 4, 2: 193-214.

Office of Technology Assessment (OTA) (1978) Assessing the Efficacy and Safety of Medical Technologies. Washington, DC: Government Printing Office.

PATTON, M. Q. (1978) Utilization-Focused Evaluation. Beverly Hills: Sage.

SCRIVEN, M. (1974) "Evaluation perspectives and procedures," pp. 3-93 in W. J. Popham (ed.) Evaluation in Education. Berkeley: McCutchan.

SECHREST, L. and R. REDNER (1979) Strength and Integrity of Treatments in Evaluation Studies. Washington, DC: Department of Justice, LEAA.

STALLINGS, J. (1974) "An implementation study of seven Follow Through models for education." Presented at the annual meeting of the American Educational Research Association, Chicago.

WILLIAMS, W. (1976) "Implementation problems in federally funded programs," in W. Williams and R. F. Elmore (eds.) Social Program Implementation. New York: Academic Press.

——— and R. F. ELMORE [eds.] (1976) Social Program Implementation. New York: Academic Press.

6

Pat A. Thompson
American Institutes for Research

Carl D. Novak
Educational Service Unit 18

THE COMPARABILITY OF TEST RESULTS AGGREGATED ACROSS TEST BATTERIES

In conducting large-scale evaluation studies, it is frequently necessary to aggregate results from different test batteries. An issue that must be addressed in evaluation studies where multiple tests are used is whether the tests and test results are, in fact, comparable. This can be a problem any time multiple tests are used interchangeably; each student takes only one test or test battery, and selection and administration of the tests are not determined on a random basis. In evaluation of Title I programs, the local districts select and administer the tests and submit the data to the state for aggregation. Thus, the evaluation of Title I programs, which is the focus of this chapter, provides an excellent example where the issue of the comparability of tests and test results is central.

THE TITLE I EVALUATION AND REPORTING SYSTEM

Over fifteen years have passed since the passage of the Elementary and Secondary Education Act and still Congress has yet to receive data on a nationwide basis on the effectiveness of Title I programs in impacting achievement. However, Congress will soon be receiving the first report based on nationwide data largely resulting from national use of the Title I Evaluation and Reporting System (TIERS). TIERS was developed to meet the requirements of the 1974 Amendments to the Elementary and Secondary Education Act. It represents an attempt to standardize local evaluation and reporting practices so that Title I impact data can be systematically collected and aggregated at the state and national levels and thus be available for decision-making. Stated by Bessey et al. (1975: 5):

> The Title I evaluation and reporting system was developed to provide meaningful and comparable information on all Title I projects throughout the country and to permit aggregation of this information at the school, district, state, and Federal levels.

TIERS consists of three evaluation models or strategies which yield achievement data expressed in terms of a common metric called Normal Curve Equivalent scores or simply NCEs. The NCE scale is like a percentile scale in that it has values of "1" and "99" at the extremes, and "50" is the midpoint of the distribution. However, the NCE scale is different in that it is an equal interval scale with equal distances between individual scale points. Thus, NCE scores can be averaged across students, districts, or states even when the NCEs are based on results from different test batteries.

Most districts use the norm referenced model with nationally standardized and normed tests (Model A-1) for evaluation of their Title I programs. In this model, Title I students are given an achievement pretest and posttest, usually during the same academic year. Pretest and posttest percentile scores are computed using the appropriate norms tables and the percentile scores are then converted into NCE scores. NCE gains from pretest to posttest represent the impact of the Title I program on the achievement of Title I students. The requirements for implementing Model A-1 (Tallmadge and Wood, 1978) are summarized as follows:

- The test administered should have national norms; or if the test has only local norms, then a test with national norms must also be given or must be previously available.
- The pretest achievement score should not be used as the basis for selecting students for Title I participation.
- The pretest and posttest should be given within two weeks of the midpoint of the dates during which the test was normed.
- The pretest and posttest should be comparable. This means the same test and subtest should be given for both testings and, if possible, the same test levels and forms should be given.

- The selected test levels should be appropriate for the functioning level of the students.
- The impact of the program on student achievement should only be evaluated for students with a gain score (that is, students with both pretest and posttest scores).

None of the evaluation models of TIERS, including Model A-1, specifies that a particular test or set of tests be used in measuring the impact of the Title I program on achievement.

There has been much debate and research related to TIERS since its development. Most of this debate and research has focused on the comparability of the three evaluation models, the assumption that students will perform at the same percentile from pre- to posttesting without Title I assistance (that is, equipercentile assumption) and the effects of violating various requirements (implementation rules) of the models. There is little research relevant to the basic assumption underlying TIERS that commonly used standardized tests are sufficiently comparable to allow aggregation of scores across tests, even though this is an assumption central to the system.

RESEARCH ON THE
COMPARABILITY OF TEST BATTERIES

There is a scarcity of research and literature on the comparability of test batteries. After exhaustive manual and computer searches, Buckley (1981) found little research material in this area. Many of the research studies comparing the difficulty of various test batteries were completed during the 1960s and involved comparing grade-equivalent scores obtained by a select group of students on two to five test batteries (Tait, 1955; Stake, 1961; Taylor and Crandall, 1962; Finley, 1963; Millman and Lindlof, 1964; Davis, 1971, 1968; Anastasiow, 1969; Goolsby, 1971). These studies generally involved administering the test batteries to the same group of students or to students matched on variables such as IQ. Comparability of the tests was determined by analysis of grade-equivalent scores from the tests, particularly by correlating pairs of test results. Unfortunately, most of the editions of the tests included in these studies are now obsolete, and the comparisons were based on grade-equivalent scores.

The largest comparative study of achievement tests conducted to date is the Anchor Test Study which was completed by contract from the Office of Education (now the U.S. Department of Education).

The major purposes of the study were to provide equivalency tables that would allow translation of scores on any one of eight standardized tests to other tests, and to provide new national norms for these tests. Tables were produced for the reading subtest for grades 4, 5, and 6 (Loret et al., 1974). Based on the results of the Anchor Test Study, some authors argue that the tests are quite comparable (Silberberg and Silberberg, 1977) while others (Jaeger, n.d.: 89) argue that "mean differences on each of the tests cannot be considered to be equivalent, nor can effectiveness results from projects that used different reading comprehension tests be considered comparable." It would seem, however, that the perceived need for the equivalency tables produced by the study is based on the assumption that test results are not sufficiently comparable to begin with.

Given that tests are probably not sufficiently comparable to allow aggregation of data across tests, the idea of selecting one instrument, or several carefully equated instruments, for national use has been considered. Imposing use of one or a few instruments on Local Educational Agencies (LEAs) would certainly make TIERS more straightforward and statistically more sound. In developing and disseminating TIERS, however, the Office of Education (now the U.S. Department of Education) wanted a system that would provide valid evaluation data for use at the LEA level, and this probably would not be the case if LEAs were mandated to use particular tests (Stonehill and Fishbein, 1979). As stated by Tallmadge and Horst (1978: 12), "We are firmly convinced that the system as it is currently designed, will yield a much fairer assessment of what Title I is accomplishing than could be obtained using a single test to assess all treatments."

THE PURPOSE OF THIS STUDY

The purpose of the present study was to address two major questions of practical relevance to Title I evaluation. The issues addressed here were conceptually different than those addressed in previous research, although the differences may appear subtle. The questions addressed were, "Do the tests most commonly used for Title I evaluation yield comparable results?" and "Do individual tests yield consistent results across locations (states) and time (fiscal years)?"

The first research question focuses on the comparability of *test results,* unlike earlier research that focuses on the comparability of *tests*. As previously mentioned, the scanty literature available in this area usually compared a small number of tests from a correlational point of view. The correlations between test scores only indicated where students scored in the distributions, regardless of how the score distributions were anchored. In other words, correlations between test scores do not provide information about the relative difficulty of the tests or the comparability of test results. The correlations between results on two tests could be quite high even when Test A yields low scores and Test B yields high scores. Especially in reference to gain scores, which are used to measure impact in Title I, the comparability of tests and the comparability of results from tests address two different issues.

The second research question focuses separately on each of the most commonly used tests to determine if the tests yield consistent results across several states and two fiscal years. If the tests do yield consistent results across these two dimensions, then more powerful, practical recommendations about use of the tests for Title I evaluation can be made. For example, if Test A yields high pretest scores consistently across different states and during different fiscal years, then one could make a strong recommendation for use of Test A when high pretest scores are desirable. The strength and generalizability of the recommendations which can be made from any study are dependent on the replicability of the results across location and time.

This study was not designed to critically investigate TIERS, the comparability assumption underlying TIERS, the NCE scale, or use of different test batteries. Instead, the study investigated the comparability of test results, *given* that TIERS is used, NCEs are used, different tests are used, and that mandating standard use of one or more tests is not a good idea. The goal of the study was to develop practical recommendations regarding results from different test batteries which can be expected within TIERS. For example, in selecting a test for Title I evaluation purposes, it would be very useful to know what kinds of gains are generally obtained from various test batteries.

Teachers, administrators, and other district personnel often hold subjective impressions regarding the relative nature of scores obtained using various tests. Working in the area of Title I evaluation, it is not uncommon to hear comments among teachers such as "I use Test X for selection because it is so hard that students score low, and so we can select more students into the program" or "Don't use Test Y because students do well on it and so their gains look bad.'' What is remarkable is that teachers, who usually give the tests and supposedly use the test results, do hold similar subjective impressions about relative performance on various test batteries. What is needed is empirical documentation of the degree to which test results are consistent across test using a large amount of actual Title I data from several states and years.

In an attempt to answer these research questions and to derive useful recommendations, special effort was made in this study to include as much quality data as possible. The results of many studies using Title I evaluation data are not generalizable and/or useful because the studies do not carefully select data for inclusion in the study. In this study, an attempt was made to control the data included in the analysis based on the results of prior research. For example, experience and research have repeatedly shown that NCE gains are usually higher for math than reading and that NCE gain scores are usually higher for fall-to-spring evaluations compared to spring-to-spring or fall-to-fall evaluations (see Thompson and Novak, 1980). Given these consistent findings, this study included separate analyses of math and reading data from fall-to-spring evaluations only. As presented later, other project and testing characteristics known to affect test results were also controlled in this study in an attempt to more accurately investigate the research questions of interest.

In summary, the purpose of the study is to investigate to what extent test batteries commonly used within the Title I Evaluation and Reporting system do yield comparable results (that is, give the same estimate of program effect). Where systematic differences due to test battery are evident, the chapter will explore how the differences might be explained.

DESCRIPTION OF DATA USED IN THE STUDY

The data used in the study were generously provided by four states in the Midwest and were from two fiscal years, FY1979 and FY1980. A total of six data sets were used. The size of the six data sets ranged from about 21,000 student records to about 98,000 student records. The average amount of data across the data sets was over 43,000 student records per set; the median was about 34,000 records. However, only a relatively small subset of the available data was used for this study. All of the data sets included data for almost all Title I students in the state during the year with the exception of the smallest data set which contained about two-thirds of all possible student data.

Most of the data sets consisted of individual student records with the exception of one data set which consisted of records with data aggregated across students. The data sets also differed in the manner by which raw test scores were converted into percentiles and then were converted into NCE scores. For one data set, NCEs were submitted directly by the local district. For two other data sets, raw scores were submitted by the districts and were converted into NCE scores by a computer program using the test information provided and test norm table files. For the remaining four data sets, the districts submitted percentile scores which were then simply converted to NCE scores. Although the record types and the method by which NCE scores were calculated differed across data sets, all data sets included NCE scores and information for the variables of descriptive interest in this study.

Data analyzed in an attempt to answer the research questions were carefully selected based on several important project and testing characteristics. The characteristics were selected from findings of previous research and from the implementation rules underlying Model A-1. Controlling for important project and testing characteristics yielded more precisely defined and homogeneous sets of data for use in investigating the research questions.

In terms of project characteristics, data from only pull-out reading or math programs in grades two through six were included. Reading and math data were always analyzed separately. In addition, only data for students who were in the Title I program for at least 50 instructional hours were included in the analyses. Table 6.1 shows that all four project characteristics were used to select data based on all project characteristics for the remaining data sets because needed information was not available.

Data were also selected based on research or on the degree of compliance with several implementation rules of the TIERS models. First of all, only student data where a gain score could be calculated were included. This requirement implies that the student had to be in the Title I program at least six months. Second, only data from a fall-to-spring testing interval were selected. Since research has repeatedly shown that test results vary depending on the testing interval used, the testing interval was held constant. Other testing rquirements were that the same test and subtest were given for the pretest and posttest to help

TABLE 6.1
Project and Student Characteristics Used in Selected Data From Six Data Sets

	DATA SET[a]					
	A-79	A-80	B-79	B-80	C-80	D-79
PROJECT CHARACTERISTICS						
1. Reading and Math programs	X	X	X	X	X[b]	X
2. Grades 2 through 6	X	X	X	X	X	X
3. Only pull-out programs	X	X	X	X		X
4. At least 50 total hours of instructional time	X	X	X	X		X
TESTING CHARACTERISTICS						
5. Have a gain score (so took both tests)	X	X	X	X	X	X
6. Fall to Spring test interval	X	X	X	X	X	X
7. Same test pre to post	X	X	X	X	X[c]	X
8. Same subtest pre to post	X		X	X		X
9. Tested within 30 absolute days of norming dates	X	X	X	X		X
10. Not selected using pretest			X	X		X
11. Both tests given inlevel				X		

Note: [a] The letters A to D represent the four states while 79 and 80 represent FY1979 and FY1980 respectively.

[b] Data for Language Arts students were included with Reading student data.

[c] Assumed same test was given but could not be empirically checked.

ensure comparability. Also, the two testing must have been within 30 total absolute days of the appropriate norm dates. One implementation rule of TIERS is that the tests must be given within a period ± two weeks of the empirical norm dates. Data were selected from all but one data set based on all five of these criteria. Finally, data were omitted from analysis if the pretest was used for selection and/or if out-of-level testing was used when it was possible to use these criteria as well (when the needed information was available). Selection based on the pretest is known to affect gain scores used to estimate the impact of Title I on achievement (Roberts, 1981). Administration of in-level versus out-of-level testing is also known to affect achievement results (Jaeger, undated); therefore, test results should not be pooled across these two administrations. Table 6.1 displays which testing characteristics were used in selecting data from each of the data sets. Again, the purpose of selecting data meeting a well-defined set of project and testing characteristics was to analyze carefully defined and more homogeneous data.

FREQUENCY OF TEST BATTERY USAGE

How many tests are commonly used?

A first phase of analyses was run on reading and math data separately to determine which test batteries were given for Title I evaluation purposes. These descriptive analyses included all data for students in grades 2 through 6 who had gain scores. The analyses provided descriptive information regarding test usage and determined which tests would be looked at more closely in the second phase of analyses addressing the research questions.

The first phase of analyses indicated that only five or six tests (mode = 6 tests) were completed by over 80 percent of the reading students in a state for a given year. In math, from four to seven tests (mode = 5 tests) were completed by 80 percent of the total math students depending upon the data set (state and year). This is an important finding indicating that, although the local districts could use any of a large number of tests in the states providing data for this study, only a relatively small number of tests were actually given to most students. This is encouraging since it implies that investigating the consistency of results for only a few most commonly used tests will account for the tests taken by a majority of students. The findings also suggests that if Title I evaluation practices are standardized to the point where LEAs can use only one of several achievement tests, then many districts would probably not need to change the tests they are using. In other words, it appears that mandating use of a few selected tests may not require a change in testing practices for a large number of districts.

Which tests are commonly used?

The reading and math test batteries given to at least 80 percent of the students from each data set are listed in Tables 6.2 and 6.3. The tables contain the percentage of students who took the test battery and the test rank within the data set. Some commonality in test battery usage across the states and the two years can be seen.

Excluding cases where it was uncertain which test edition was given, a total of 11 different test batteries were given to 80 percent or more reading students from the six individual data sets (Table 6.2). The most frequently used tests for reading students were the 1965 and 1978 editions of the Gates-MacGinitie Reading Test (GMRT). Other frequently used tests were the 1973 edition of the Stanford Achievement Test (SAT 73), the Stanford Diagnostic Reading Test (SDRT 76), and the Metropolitan Achievement Test (MAT 70).

A total of ten different test batteries were given to 80 percent or more math students from the six individual data sets, again excluding cases where it was uncertain which test edition was given (Table 6.3). The tests most frequently given to math students were the SAT 73, the Stanford Diagnostic Math Test (SDMT 76), and the 1970 and 1978 editions of the MAT. Another commonly used test in math was the California Achievement Test, 1977 edition (CAT 77).

THE CONSISTENCY OF TEST BATTERY RESULTS
ACROSS LOCATION AND TIME

The second phase of analyses involved selecting data from each data set which met the project and testing requirements previously described. Data were also selected only where students took one of the most commonly used test batteries relative to other tests given within the state that year. Analyses were run separately for reading and math data from each data set.

TABLE 6.2
Reading Test Batteries Most Commonly Used in Grades Two Through Six by Data Set

	DATA SET[a]											
	A-79		A-80		B-79		B-80		C-80		D-79	
	rank	%	rank	%	rank	%	rank	%	rank	%	rank	%
CAT[b]									1	24.3%		
CAT 77			5	8.9%					2	22.3%		
GMRT[b]												
GMRT 65	1	19.8%	3	12.0%	1	32.5%	6	6.1%			2	19.3%
GMRT 78	3	17.4%	1	26.5%	2	21.3%	1	48.0%			4	6.5%
ITBS 71											1	29.2%
MAT[b]												
MAT 70	4	15.7%	6	6.3%	3	12.5%	3	9.1%	6	5.5%		
MAT/S78					5	7.0%	2	9.9%				
SAT 73	6	6.0%			4	10.4%	4	7.8%	3	14.6%	3	13.8%
SDRT 76	5	7.6%	4	10.3%			5	6.6%	5	7.3%	5	6.0%
SRA[b]	2	18.7%	2	17.4%								
SRA ACH 71											7	3.8%
SRA ACH 78											6	5.9%
Woodcock 73									4	11.4%		

Note: These data are based on students who had gain scores.

[a] The letters A through D represent the four states, while 79 and 80 represent FY1979 and FY1980 respectively.

[b] It was not possible to determine which edition of these tests were used, so this information is kept separate.

TABLE 6.3
Math Test Batteries Most Commonly Used in Grades Two Through Six by Data Set

	DATA SET[a]											
	A-79		A-80		B-79		B-80		C-80		D-79	
	rank	%	rank	%	rank	%	rank	%	rank	%	rank	%
CAT[b]									1	31.0%		
CAT 77			7	4.4%	5	12.0%	4	15.3%			4	8.1%
ITBS 71											1	29.0%
Keymath 76									4	10.9%		
MAT[b]									5	5.5%		
MAT 70	2	22.5%	3	12.0%	1	25.3%	2	17.6%				
MAT 78			4	7.6%								
MAT/178											5	7.7%
MAT/S78					3	19.5%	1	27.2%				
SAT 73	4	9.0%	6	6.4%	2	20.9%	3	16.2%	2	21.3%	2	18.9%
SDMT 76	3	14.3%	2	16.4%	4	12.7%	5	13.9%	3	14.5%	3	11.9%
SRA[b]	1	35.6%	1	28.5%								
SRA ACH 71											6	6.0%
WRAT[b]			5	7.0%								

Note: These data are based on students who had gain scores.

[a] The letters A through D represent the four states, while 79 and 80 represent FY1979 and FY1980 respectively.

[b] It was not possible to determine which edition of these tests were used, so this information is kept separate.

Mean pretest, posttest, and gain NCE scores were calculated by grade for particular subtests of each commonly used test battery. For most reading tests, mean NCE scores were based only on student data from the Total Reading subtest. In a few cases where Total Reading scores were not available for all grades of focus, either Total Reading or Comprehension subtest scores were used. Only Total Math subtest scores were selected for the analyses of the math data. Analyses were limited to Total Reading, Reading Comprehension, or Total Math subtests because scores from these subtests are generally the most reliable.

Results from many of the frequently used test batteries dropped out of this second phase of analyses because of the stringent requirements used for data selection. For example, 46.9 percent of SDRT 76 scores were lost from one data set when student selection based on the pretest was used for omitting data. Thus, results based on a sufficient sample size were not available for all of the frequently used tests from each data set.

Reading: Overall Test Results

Mean NCE gains across data sets for the five most commonly used test batteries in reading are presented at the top of Table 6.4. Data were collapsed across grades 2 through 6 in this presentation. These means were based on sample sizes ranging from 167 to 4103 student records per cell with an average cell sample size of 1000 (median N was 885). Pretest NCE scores for these same students are presented in Table 6.5. The pretest information gives more meaning to interpreting the gains because it offers a common starting point for comparing test results. For example, large gain scores may be primarily due to students performing very poorly on the pretest *or* students performing very well on the posttest. Having information about pretest performance allows more meaningful interpretation of the gain scores. Although pretest scores were not statistically compared for each test, it appears that there were no blatant systematic biases in the mean pretest NCEs as a function of test battery.

The mean NCE reading gains for the five test batteries are also presented in Figure 6.1. Inspection of Table 6.4 and Figure 6.1 indicates that mean NCE gains for the GMRT 65 and GMRT 78 reading tests were relatively stable across five different data sets from three states. In addition, overall means from the GMRT 78 were usually

TABLE 6.4
Mean NCE Gains Across Six Data Sets for The Most Commonly Used Test Batteries

READING TESTS

					DATA SET[a]							
	A-79		A-80		B-79		B-80		C-80		D-79	
	$\overline{X}$	(SD)	$\overline{X}$	(SD)	$\overline{X}$	(SD)	$\overline{X}$	(SD)	$\overline{X}$	(SD)	$\overline{X}$	(SD)
GMRT 65	6.25	(12.7)	6.79	(11.5)	4.57	(13.8)	5.81	(14.6)	—	—	6.81	(15.8)
GMRT 78	8.80	(12.0)	8.01	(11.8)	9.37	(12.3)	6.57	(10.7)	—	—	6.36	(12.8)
MAT 70	6.43	(11.6)	6.58	(10.4)	6.96	(12.1)	2.56	(11.2)	—	—	—	—
SAT 73	6.06	(9.8)	—	—	—	—	5.27	(10.0)	7.94	(12.2)	5.88	(13.8)
SDRT 76	11.85	(14.0)	14.47	(16.5)	—	—	7.53	(12.4)	11.75	(13.6)	9.76	(15.8)

MATH TESTS

	A-79		A-80		B-79		B-80		C-80		D-79	
	$\overline{X}$	(SD)	$\overline{X}$	(SD)	$\overline{X}$	(SD)	$\overline{X}$	(SD)	$\overline{X}$	(SD)	$\overline{X}$	(SD)
SDMT 76	15.78	(15.4)	14.21	(12.7)	5.20	(12.7)	7.40	(11.1)	11.68	(15.1)	10.52	(15.9)
SAT 73	7.28	(10.7)	—	—	—	—	—	—	11.84	(13.8)	8.48	(15.7)
MAT 70	9.41	(11.2)	7.47	(12.9)	—	—	—	—	—	—	—	—
CAT 77	—	—	—	—	7.27	(13.3)	9.75	(12.2)	—	—	8.48	(14.8)

Note: The letters A through D represent the four states, while 79 and 80 represent FY1979 and FY1980 respectively.

TABLE 6.5

Mean Pretest NCEs Across Six Data Sets for The Most Commonly Used Test Batteries

| | DATA SET[a] | | | | | | | | | | | |
| | A-79 | | A-80 | | B-79 | | B-80 | | C-80 | | D-79 | |
	$\overline{X}$	(SD)	$\overline{X}$	(SD)	$\overline{X}$	(SD)	$\overline{X}$	(SD)	$\overline{X}$	(SD)	$\overline{X}$	(SD)
READING TESTS												
GMRT 65	35.49	(11.4)	36.49	(11.0)	37.86	(15.4)	38.38	(15.0)	—		34.46	(34.7)
GMRT 78	33.62	(10.7)	35.06	(11.4)	36.63	(13.9)	36.63	(13.1)	—		30.43	(33.0)
MAT 70	36.51	(10.8)	37.58	(9.0)	35.17	(13.2)	34.50	(18.0)	—		—	
SAT 73	39.54	(10.6)	—		—		37.93	(17.1)	31.40	(15.4)	36.52	(37.7)
SDRT 76	37.02	(10.5)	35.92	(13.1)	—		39.98	(13.4)	36.46	(13.7)	37.59	(37.3)
MATH TESTS												
SDMT 76	38.77	(13.5)	35.65	(13.2)	37.70	(11.7)	38.64	(11.5)	34.99	(13.4)	36.23	(36.9)
SAT 73	34.27	(12.1)	—		—		38.25	(8.6)	28.25	(13.8)	37.21	(36.9)
MAT 70	34.44	(10.4)	37.15	(9.5)	—		34.63	(18.8)	—		—	
CAT 77	—		—		44.13	(13.7)	44.90	(12.3)	—		32.27	(37.6)

Note: The letters A through D represent the four states, while 79 and 80 represent FY1979 and FY1980 respectively.

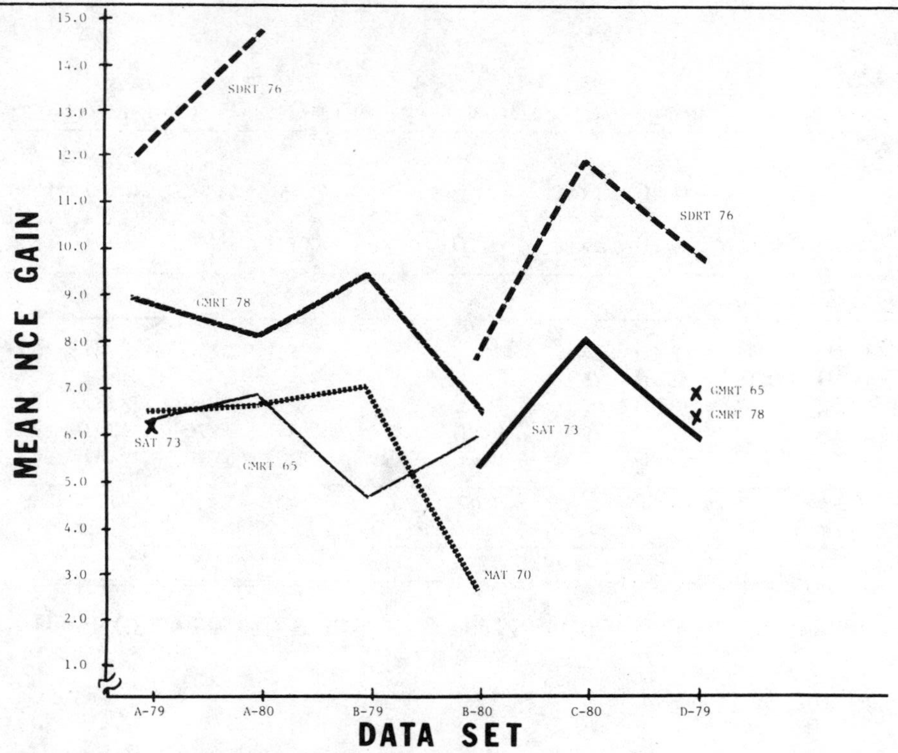

Figure 6.1 Mean NCE Reading Gains by Data Set for Commonly Used Test Batteries

higher than means from the earlier 1965 edition of the same test. This was a consistent finding across two years of data from two states. In fact, on the average across five data sets, gains from the GMRT 78 were about two NCEs higher than gains from the same data sets from the 1965 edition of the GMRT. It is not clear why this result was found.

The most interesting finding regarding NCE reading gains as a function of test used concerned SDRT 76 results. Mean NCE gains from the SDRT 76 were much higher for each of the five data sets when compared with gains from the four other tests. Out of the 29 possible comparisons of gains from the SDRT 76 with gains from the other tests, NCE gains from the SDRT 76 were always higher. Although this appears to be an exciting finding with practical implications, a caution is in order.

Spring norms for the SDRT 76 were published separately from the test manuals in 1978 "Supplementary Norms Booklets." As a result, many districts did not have spring norms for the SDRT 76 test and, fall norms from the original norms tables were used instead for both the fall and spring conversions. When this is the case, it is no wonder that the districts had large positive gains. This problem became evident in an earlier study by the authors (Thompson and Novak, 1980). When a subset of the data from the earlier study were checked manually for conversion errors, a large number of districts had, in fact, used fall norms for their spring conversions. In addition, there is evidence from the current study that SDRT 76 gains were not unusually large and positive relative to other tests when all fall and spring conversions were done by computer. For these reasons, relatively large positive gains from the SDRT 76 may be due more to incorrect score conversions than to characteristics of the test.

Reading: Test Results by Grade

Reading test scores were also analyzed by grade to investigate the consistency of test results as a function of the students' grade level. In general, NCE gains from Title I programs were positive and relatively large at the lower elementary grades and tended to decrease as a function of grade level. Analyses performed by grade provided an opportunity to determine if trends such as these were more predominant for some tests than others. Analyses by grade may also indicate changes in test results which are due to different test levels, since these are grade-related (such as a switch from elementary to intermediate level at grade 5). Data from students in grades 2 through 6 meeting the requirements previously discussed were included in these analyses.

Analyses of reading test results by grade produced results with a "sufficient" sample size per cell from two or more data sets for three test batteries: (1) GMRT 65, (2) GMRT 78, and (3) SDRT 76. The term "sufficient" used in the context of the reading analyses refers to sample sizes per cell of at least 100 students. For example, all 25 cells for the GMRT 78 analyses (5 grades $\times$ 5 data sets = 25) had sample sizes ranging from 141 to 462 with an average cell size of about 269 students. Out of the grade total of 65 cells reported for the second phase of reading analyses, only three cells had sample sizes slightly less than 100; but these were not omitted from the reading analyses. Results for each of the three test batteries for which sufficient data were available will be presented separately.

Gates-MacGinitie Reading Test, 1965 edition. There was sufficient data for each grade across five data sets (representing 3 states) for reading students who took the GMRT 65 test. The mean NCE gains for the GMRT 65 across grades 2 through 6 and for each data set are displayed in Figure 6.2. Mean gains from this test were fairly consistent across the five data sets for most grades except for grade 2. The average NCE gains were particularly consistent across data sets for grades 3 and 5. For grade 2, mean gains varied by as much as seven NCEs for different data sets. In addition, these data did not suggest a decrease in NCE gains as a function of grade level. In fact, a small increase in gains from grades 4 through 6 can be seen in Figure 6.2. This increase may be due to the fact that, beginning at grade 4, the in-level test ("Survey D" level) is the same for all three of these grades.

These findings suggest that gains from the GMRT 65 test do not tend to decrease from grades 2 through 6, but tend to be fairly consistent across most grades. For grade 2,however, mean NCE gains appear less stable. When interpreting the results from the GMRT 65 test, it is important to remember that gains from this test appear to be consistently smaller than those obtained using the more recent edition of the Gates-MacGinitie Reading Test.

Gates-MacGinitie Reading Test, 1978. Sufficient data for each grade across five data sets (representing three states) were also available for the 1978 edition of the GMRT. As can be seen in Figure 6.3, NCE gain score for the 1978 edition were less stable across data

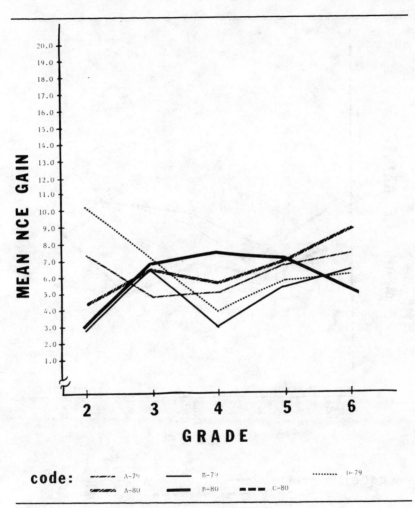

Figure 6.2   Mean NCE Reading Gains for the GMRT 65

sets than were gain scores from the earlier edition. However, NCE gains from the GMRT 78 were quite consistent across sets for grades 2 and 3. At grade 4, two FY1979 data sets had larger mean gains than three other data sets which were similar to one another. In other words, while results for the GMRT 78 were fairly consistent for grades 2 and 3, they diverged at grade 4.

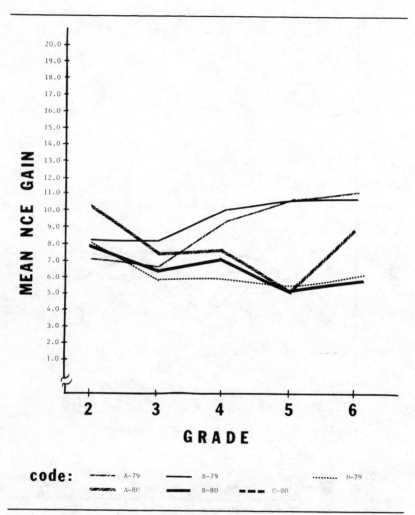

MEAN NCE GAIN (y-axis)

GRADE (x-axis)

code: A-79   B-79   D-79
       A-80   B-80   C-80

Figure 6.3 Mean NCE Reading Gains for the GMRT 78

In this study the NCE gains based on the GMRT 78 tended to be positive and larger than gains based on other commonly used tests. Mean gains across grades were fairly stable for this test for grades 2 and 3. However, the magnitude of gains from the GMRT 78 appeared to be less stable for grades 4, 5, and 6.

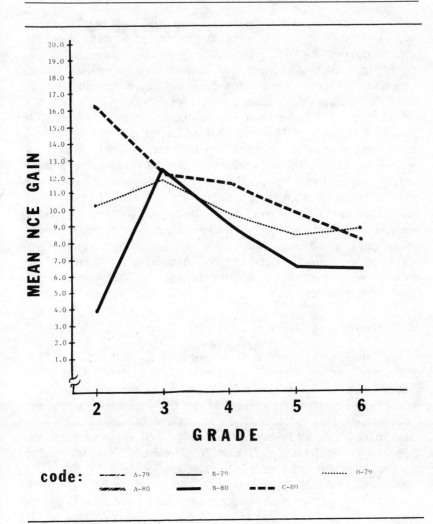

Figure 6.4   Mean NCE Reading Gains for the SDRT 76

Stanford Diagnostic Reading Test, 1976. A total of three data sets from three different states had sufficient SDRT 76 data at each grade. The mean NCE gains for the SDRT 76 are presented in Figure 6.4. The results across grades 3 through 6 were fairly stable and showed a constant downward trend as grade level increased. This was the only reading tests out of three being discussed where mean gains did decrease as a function of grade level.

The results at grade 2 showed variability with a range of from 4.0 NCEs to 16.0 NCEs for the two extreme mean gain scores. Based on results from the SDRT 76 and a familiarity with the data sets involved, this finding was most likely due to incorrect score conversions. When a computer program converted raw scores into NCEs using the appropriate norm tables in computer files, mean NCE gains were lower for almost every grade. For grade 2, the mean NCE gain was about 4.0 compared to gains of 10.0 and 16.0 NCEs for the data sets where scores were manually converted. Usually, the closer the evaluation system used at the local and state levels resembles the implementation and reporting criteria specified by TIERS, the smaller (and more realistic?) the gain estimates are. Even given that the large mean NCE gains from the SDRT 76 were primarily due to conversion errors, it was still unclear why SDRT 76 results were consistent across all grades except grade 2. Perhaps using fall norms for both fall and spring norms inflates gains more at the early elementary grades because these are the grades where the larger gains are realized. Even if this is true, however, it still does not explain why grade 2 results were so deviant.

Math: Overall Test Results

The consistency of mean NCE gains across data sets for four commonly used math tests are presented in Figure 6.5. Data from grades 2 through 6 were collapsed in this presentation. The emphasis was on looking for consistency across the various data sets for frequently used test batteries. These means were based on sample sizes ranging from 165 to 1946 student records per cell with an average cell sample size of 556 (median N was 320). Pretest NCE means for the same students with math gains are included in Table 6.5.

Inspection of Table 6.5 indicates that overall mean NCE gains for the SDMT 76 were generally larger than those for the other three test batteries, except when score conversions were done by computer. It appears that the problem previously discussed in reference to the SDRT 76 also applies to the SDMT 76. In fact, results from the SDMT 76 provide further evidence in support of the comments made regarding SDRT 76 results.

Overall mean gains for the CAT 77 differed by about 1.3 NCEs for two data sets representing two states and two years. For the SAT 73, the average difference in NCEs for three data sets from three states was 3.0 NCEs. For the two data sets from the same state, the NCE

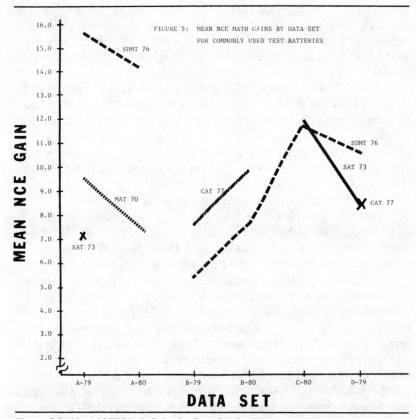

Figure 6.5   Mean NCE Math Gains by Data Set for Commonly Used Test Batteries

difference on the MAT 70 was 1.9 NCEs. In general, overall mean NCE gains in math for the CAT 77, SAT 73, and MAT 70 were not widely different from each other even across four states and two years. In addition, overall means for the SDMT 76 would likely be similar for all data sets if the conversion of spring scores were done correctly.

Math: Test Result by Grade

Analyses of math tests results yielded small sample sizes for some grades by data cells, even for commonly used math tests. For the most frequently used math test, the SDMT 76, the sample sizes for the 20 cells ranged from only 38 to 267, although the average cell size was 116 students. For this reason, math results by grade will be briefly presented. The unequal and small cell sample sizes should be considered in interpreting the results of the math analyses by test and grade.

For the SDMT 76, mean NCE gains by grade were plotted for four data sets from three states. The average gains from the SDMT 76 were not only large relative to other math tests, but they were also inconsistent within and across data sets. For one data set, a difference of about 11 mean NCEs was found for grade 2 compared with grade 6. Across data sets, mean NCEs differed by as much as 13 NCEs. The inconsistencies across data sets for the SDMT 76 may be partially due to the small cell sample sizes on which the means were based.

Mean NCE gains based on SAT 73 math results from two data sets (representing two states) were not similar. For the data set with a very large sample size per cell, mean gains from the SAT 73 decreased slightly in a consistent manner as the grade level increased. However, for the data set with very small cell sample sizes, a "U"-shaped function of mean scores across grades became evident.

Mean NCE gains based on the CAT 77 from two data sets (representing two states) decreased sharply and consistently from grades 2 through 4. A decrease in mean NCE gains as grade level increased was more evident for this test than for the earlier tests which have been discussed. For grades 5 and 6, the results differed somewhat for the two data sets. Again, inconsistencies found in the math data may be due to small sample sizes and should be interpreted cautiously.

SUMMARY

Large data sets from four states and from fiscal years 1979 and 1980 were analyzed to investigate the consistency of Title I evaluation results for commonly used test batteries. Where consistencies or differences due to test battery were found, attempts were made to explain these results. Data included in the study were carefully selected based on project and testing characteristics identified as important in the literature or which are part of the implementation requirements of the Title I Evaluation and Reporting System.

The first phase of analyses provided information on the frequency of test battery usage for students in grades 2 through 6. The results indicated that, although numerous tests could be used, a very few test batteries account for 80 percent or more of the tests administered to the students. In measuring the impact of Title I on student achievement, reading students were most frequently given the GMRT 65, GMRT 78, SAT 73, SDRT 76, or the MAT 70. Math students were most frequently given the SAT 73, SDMT 76, MAT 70, MAT 78 Instructional or Survey batteries, or CAT 77.

The second phase of analyses included data from each data set which met strict project and testing criteria. Reading and math mean NCE gain scores were presented by data set to provide an overall descriptive comparison of gains as a function of test battery. Mean NCE gains were then presented separately by data set by grade for several of the most commonly used tests. These descriptive analyses explored the consistency of results for individual test batteries.

One of the major findings from the second phase of analyses was that mean NCE gains from the SDRT 76 and SDMT 76 were often very large and positive relative to other tests, but probably were mostly the result of incorrect conversion of spring test scores. It appeared that gains from the SDRT 76 and SDMT 76 were much more comparable to those from other tests when score conversions were based on the appropriate norms.

Another major finding was that the 1978 edition of the GMRT appeared to yield larger gains than the 1965 edition of the same test. This was a consistent finding across two years of data from two states.

Descriptive analyses of mean NCE gains by grade indicated that gains from the GMRT 65 were fairly consistent across five data sets (representing three states) for all grades except grade 2. Mean NCE gains for the GMRT 78 were less stable, although they were quite consistent across data sets for grades 2 and 3. The SDRT 76 yielded mean NCE gains which were fairly stable across grades 3 through 6 and which showed a constant downward trend as grade level increased. The SDRT 76 was the only reading test out of the three discussed where gains showed a consistent decrease as a function of grade level.

Overall NCE gains in math were generally larger for the SDMT 76 than for three other commonly used test batteries, except when score conversions were done by computer. Results from the SDMT 76 support comments made regarding SDRT 76 results.

CONCLUSIONS

The results of the study indicate that different test batteries produce fairly similar estimates of gains and pretest scores across data sets representing different locations (states) and times (fiscal years). Of the 23 mean gains by data set for five commonly used reading tests, 19 fell within a four NCE rance from 5.0 to 9.0 NCEs (see Table 5.3). Of the 23 mean gains, 11 fell within a two NCE range from 6.0 to 8.0 NCEs. The differences among test battery results which were found were generally small considering the data and methodology used, and were not consistent across state of year. The one exception was the SDRT 76. Reading gains from the SDRT 76 were substantially larger than gains from all other reading tests. The larger gain scores were primarily due to manual conversion of posttest raw scores to percentile scores using incorrect norms tables. SDRT 76 gains were most comparable to estimates of gain from other tests when raw scores were converted at the SEA level by a computer program containing the correct norm tables. Analysis of the math data yielded similar findings for the SDMT 76.

Although the results of the study generally support the aggregation of data across test batteries, they should be interpreted cautiously for several reasons. First of all, even if consistent differences in gains are found in a study such as this, it is uncertain whether they are due to characteristics of the test battery. That is one reason why precautions were made to carefully select a homogeneous set of data for analysis in this study. Still, since test use by the local districts was not randomly determined, it is possible that test results were due to the program or treatment effects rather than to test characteristics. There is no reason to believe, however, that projects using particular tests are any more effective in affecting student achievement than projects using other tests.

Second, the study focused on six reading tests and four math tests which are commonly used in Title I evaluation. All of the batteries were high quality, nationally normed, standardized tests administered to a majority of the students within each data set. A relatively large number of tests, however, were administered to the remaining students, but were not included in this study. Although it is likely that the tests included in the study are in many respects similar to each other, they are not necessarily similar to tests excluded from the study. Even though consistent results were found across tests included in the study, tests excluded from the study may or may not produce consistent results.

Third, another potential problem in any study using actual TIERS data concerns the quality of the data. Errors in administering the tests, scoring the tests, making score conversions, and in reporting the results impact the study. From experience, errors such as these are typically made by certain districts and not by others; they are not random errors across projects. Since it was not possible to screen all data for errors, it is uncertain what the quality of the data was and what impact the errors may have had on results of the study. However, attempts were made to select data of quality based on project and testing characteristics and to look at data quality in explaining inconsistent results.

From a practical standpoint, the results suggest that multiple tests can be used in evaluation aimed at measuring a single outcome variable (that is, achievement gains). However, multiple tests should only be used if there is a good reason for doing so. For example, the U.S. Department of Education does not mandate use of a specific test(s) within TIERS partially because of desire to maximize the validity of test results at the LEA level and to promote local use of evaluation results. If results from multiple tests are aggregated, then at least three guidelines should be followed: (1) the tests should be parallel in purpose; (2) the tests should have national norms; and (3) the test results should be monitored by test, even when comparisons of different tests is not the focus of the evaluation.

It is important that the tests be parallel in purpose. In this study, data were aggregated separately for reading and for math and analyses were almost exclusively limited to Total Reading and Total Math subtest scores. The more similar tests are in terms of content and purpose, the more reasonable it is to aggregate results across the tests.

The decision about whether test batteries or subtests are parallel enough to make aggregation feasible is, of necessity, subjective. The decision depends on the purpose, scope, and context of the evaluation and on the content and technical characteristics of the tests.

It is also important that the tests have national norms since the norms provide the basis for aggregating results. In TIERS, only tests with empirical national norms, or tests that can be linked to other tests with empirical norms, can be used. Data should not be aggregated across tests unless the tests share logically similar norms, which can be assumed comparable, or unless the tests are empirically equated.

It is important to monitor results by test to identify potential problems, even if results by specific tests is not of interest in the study. Aberrant results from one test could have an undue influence on the overall findings of an evaluation study. Therefore, consistency of results by test should be considered any time data are aggregated across tests. If large discrepancies are evident by test, they should be addressed in the evaluation report. It is not sufficient to simply assume that the estimates across tests are comparable.

The fact that the study failed to find large inconsistencies in mean NCE gains as a function of test battery does not *prove* that the test batteries yield comparable results. There is obviously need for additional studies of TIERS data or data from other evaluation systems in which data are aggregated across multiple test batteries. Preferably, the studies will include test results which can be statistically equated (for instance, when students are double-tested) or which involve random assignment of test batteries to students. In addition, perhaps more sophisticated analyses (such as repeated measures analyses) of test data can better answer the research questions addressed in this study, at least in a quantifiable sense. Until more definitive evidence is available, however, the aggregation of data across tests appears to be defensible if reasonable caution is used in design and implementation of the evaluation study.

REFERENCES

ANASTASIOW, N. J. (1969) "Fourth through sixth grade student performance differences on STEP and SRA achievement tests" Measurement and Evaluation in Guidance 2: 149-152.

BESSY, B., L. ROSEN, A. CHIANG, and G. K. TALLMADGE (1976) "Further documentation of state ESEA Title I reporting models and their technical assistance requirements Phase I." (RMC Report No. UR 308). Mountain View, CA: RMC Research Corporation.

BUCKLEY, J. (1981) "A comparative analysis of the difficulty levels of three standardized achievement tests commonly used in ESEA Title I program evaluation." M.S. thesis, California State University at Fresno.

DAVIS, B. S. (1971) "A comparative analysis of three widely used standardized reading achievement tests for a selected group of elementary school children." Dissertation Abstracts International, 32(4831A).

DAVIS, W. Q. (1968) "A study of test score comparability among five widely used reading survey tests." Dissertation Abstracts International 29(4307A).

FINLEY, C. J. (1963) "A comparison of the California Achievement Test, Metropolitan Achievement Test and Iowa Test of Basic Skills." California Journal of Educational Research 14: 79-88.

GOOLSBY, T. M., Jr. (1971) "Appropriateness of subtests in achievement tests selection." Educational and Psychological Measurement 31: 969-972.

JAEGER, R. M. (n.d.) "On combining achievement test data through NCE scaled scores." Draft report prepared for Research Triangle Institute, Research Triangle Park, NC (USOE Contract 300-76-0096).

LORET, P., A. SEDER, J. BIANCHINI, and C. VALE (1974) Equivalence and Norms Tables for Selected Reading Achievement Tests. Berkeley, CA: Educational Testing Service.

MILLMAN, J. and J. LINDLOF (1964) "The comparability of fifth-grade norms of the California, Iowa, and Metropolitan achievement tests." Journal of Educational Measurement 1: 135-137.

ROBERTS, A. O. H. (1981) "Theoretical and empirical examinations of the regression-effect correction." Mountain View, CA: RMC Research Corporation. (draft)

SILBERBERG, N. E. and M. C. SILBERBERG (1977) "A note on reading tests and their role in defining reading difficulties." Journal of Learning Disabilities 10: 41-44.

STAKE, R. E. (1961) " 'Overestimation' of achievement with the California Achievement Test." Educational and Psychological Measurement 21: 59-62.

STONEHILL, R. M. and R. L. FISHBEIN (1979) "Summarizing the results of Title I evaluations—the comparability of achievement gains." Presented at the Conference on Large-Scale Assessment, Denver, June.

TAIT, A. T. (1955) "A comparative study of five major achievement tests." California Journal of Educational Research 6: 99-106.

TALLMADGE, G. K. and D. P. HORST (1978) "The use of different achievement tests in the ESEA Title I evaluation system." Presented at the American Educational Research Association, Toronto, March.

TALLMADGE, G. K. and C. T. WOOD (1978) "User's guide: ESEA Title I evaluation and reporting system." Prepared for U.S. Department of Health, Education, and Welfare (RMC Research Corporation).

TAYLOR, E. A. and B. H. CRANDALL (1962) "A study of the 'norm-equivalence' of certain tests approved for the California State Testing Program." California Journal of Educational Research 13: 186-192.

THOMPSON, P. and C. NOVAK (1980) "The impact of testing decisions on Title I evaluation results." Presented at the Evaluation Research Society meeting, Washington, D.C., November.

7

Richard C. Williams
Adrianne Bank
UCLA Graduate School of Education

USES OF DATA TO IMPROVE INSTRUCTION IN LOCAL SCHOOL DISTRICTS:
Problems and Possibilities

INTRODUCTION

The existence of test or evaluation data which reveal students' achievement in particular subject or skill areas does not, inevitably, lead to beneficial changes in classroom instruction and concomitant increases in student learning. We have found that without competent and sustained attention by district management to communication and supporting services, the use by principals and teachers of such data remains problematic. We believe that the naturally occurring characteristics of school organization and classroom instruction impede such use.

In this chapter, we acknowledge that research on testing and evaluation has made great advances in the past 15 years; and that other research on school and school district organization has contributed to the field's understanding of how these institutions operate. We argue that researchers must now build on these twin strands. We report on our work which is an investigation of how some school districts do, in practice, construct and maintain the needed links between their evaluation and testing activities on the one hand, and their curricular and instructional activities on the other.

AUTHORS' NOTE: Presented at the Evaluation Research Society meeting, Arlington, Virginia, November 21, 1980. The project reported here was performed pursuant to a grant from the National Institute of Education to the Center for the Study of Evaluation. However, the opinions expressed herein do not necessarily reflect the position or policy of NIE and no official endorsement should be inferred.

INTRODUCTION

Since its inception in 1972, the National Institute of Education (NIE) has supported research related to educational evaluation. Some of this research has contributed to our understanding of the ways in which evaluation and testing data can improve educational practice in American schools. From the research has emerged an important observation: The transformation of evaluation and testing results into improved school and classroom activities does not occur automatically. Instead, such transformation appears to be a complex process influenced by many factors, including the specific individuals who are expected to take action and the organizational settings within which they work.

Two large groups of individuals are potential users of testing an evaluation findings. One such group is policy makers, external to a school district who work within federal and state legislatures or agencies. Evaluators expect that large-scale evaluations of federal- or state-funded educational programs can give policy makers at these levels sound information on which to base changes in local program requirements, or to augment or cancel these programs. A second user group includes individuals internal to a school district: for example, board members, administrators, and classroom teachers. Evaluators expect that data collected about students can be of direct interest to within-district administrators and teachers who are responsible for fine-tuning their own curriculum and instructional programs.

At first glance, it would seem that the findings from any given program evaluation could be equally useful to both groups of people, each of whom could make needed policy or program modifications at their own level of authority. Such appears not to be the case. Studies by Kennedy (1980), Alkin et al. (1979), David (1978) , Patton (1978), and Weiss (1972) have found that the users' own interests and organizational settings influence the reception they give to evaluation findings. A major implication of these studies is that evaluators or test givers who expect their findings to be utilized either by distant policy makers or by local educators must attend in advance to the specific interests of these individuals and to the constraints of their organizational settings.

The Center for the Study of Evaluation (CSE), for the past five years, has been conducting research on evaluation and testing as it occurs within school districts. Our intention in this chapter is to describe school districts and the individuals who work there so as to better understand why and how the findings from evaluation and testing activities are or are not linked to instructional decision-making at the school district. First, we will provide background information on the growth of evaluation and testing; then we will make some observations on how the characteristics of school districts as organizations generally hamper the use of forms and evaluation. We will then describe our research strategy which investigates "heroic" school districts who are, in fact, using data for instructional decision-making, offer one example of such a district, and then present several elements which seem necessary in order for school districts to link evaluation and testing data with instruction.

BACKGROUND

The last 15 years have seen the growth of what might be called a testing and evaluation movement within American education. The seeds for this development had been planted decades ago when psychological, intelligence, and aptitude tests to screen and sort individuals were first developed by the military and industry. School districts subsequently followed suit. Many large school districts developed test bureaus which regularly collected and disseminated district-wide test results.

These somewhat dormant testing seedlings experienced an enormous growth spurt and change of direction when Congress passed the Elementary and Secondary Education Act in 1965. This Act required districts to provide testing and evaluation data to government agencies as a condition for continued funding. Subsequent federal and state legislation carried similar program evaluation conditions. This reporting requirement shifted the focus of testing from that of assessing individual student achievement to assessing the achievement of groups of students in a funded program. Instead of a counsellor looking at an individual's test score to assign that student to a special educational status, a funding agency would review the collectivity of scores to certify, modify, or eliminate an educational program. In short, large-scale testing of students had become one tool for generating data with which policy makers could identify, discourage, or further develop promising educational programs and practices.

The large-scale infusion of federal funds into educational evaluation since 1965 has had many additional reverberations. One important side effect of these funds is the flowering of what might be called a testing and evaluation "establishment." Elements of this evaluation "establishment" extend to school districts and include units within federal and state governments devoted to program evaluation and testing; university faculty and students engaged in courses and degree sequences in testing and evaluation; professional societies within education such as Division H of AERA, and across social action fields such as the Evaluation Research Society; and a federally funded Center for the Study of Evaluation. Inside school districts, the educational evaluation "establishment" usually consists of those testing and evaluation personnel who face the task of carrying out required evaluation and testing efforts. Centralized evaluation units in school districts have recently emerged, often composed of already employed guidance, testing, and counseling personnel. Within the last 10 years, over 400 districts have organized their testing and evaluation capabilities into research, development, and evaluation (RD&E) units which vary in size from one part-time person to dozens of professional employees (Lyon et at., 1978).

At first, academic members of the evaluation establishment outside of the school districts concentrated their attention primarily on the logic and methodology of large-scale evaluations. A prime assumption upon which many operated, even though that assumption was not always made explicit, was that federal and state policy makers were to be the prime consumers of their evaluation information; school district evaluators were expected to collect the data meticulously and accurately and to file reports. Explorations of the utilization of such data at the policy level (Boruch, 1980; Weiss, 1977) has made it increasingly clear that evaluation and testing reports as they are presently constituted do not have uniform and consistent influence on policy makers. Some reports influence some policy makers under some circumstances. At other times, the reports are used selectively to provide coroborating evidence for policy makers to justify decisions that they had already made on some other basis. And in still other instances, reports are ignored.

Concurrent with this examination of evaluation utilization by academics is interest by within-district evaluators on the utilization of testing and evaluation information (Holley, 1979). As a result, we have begun to explore whether evaluation and testing that originated as a means of satisfying the evaluation and testing concerns of external legislators and administrators could also serve as a basis for systematic and comprehensive local school district decision-making.

In its early days, the Center for the Study of Evaluation (CSE) (established by the same 1965 Act which attached evaluation requirements to federally funded programs) worked on the development of conceptual frameworks and technical solutions to problems of evaluation. However, in recent years, in parallel with the interest of the field, research, projects have been started which are concerned with evaluation utilization both at the school-site program administrator level (Alkin et al., 1979; Daillak, 1980) and at the school-district central office organizational level (Lyon et al., 1978). From these parallel studies of how evaluators relate to clients and of how research, development, and evaluation units handle their activities, it has become clear to us that, although the potential does exist, local utilization of evaluation and testing does not occur routinely as a natural consequence of conducting an evaluation or administering a testing program. A special combination of environmental circumstances, competent and data-oriented people, and intentional organizational arrangements seem to be required to link data collection with reporting, dissemination, and support services so as to support instructional decision-making and classroom activities.

What are the characteristics of the environment, people, and organizational arrangements that result in use of evaluation or testing data for instructional improvement? One year ago, our CSE project, officially titled "Evaluation Design: An Organizational Study," was funded by NIE to look for and study districts that were purposefully using findings from externally mandated testing or evaluation efforts in a way that influenced their instructional decision-making. Hence, the informal title of our project—"Linking Testing and Evaluation with Instruction."

From the beginning, we knew from the literature and our own research and experience in school districts that district-forged organizational links between testing, evaluation, and instruction are not commonplace. A number of the reasons offered for this nonlinkage are related to factors such as the characteristics of mandated tests and evaluations, the role or training of evaluators, technical problems with analysis, the timeliness of the reporting cycle.

We, ourselves, speculated that some of the characteristics of schools as organizations might also explain the limited use that school districts make of test and evaluation data.

SCHOOL DISTRICT CHARACTERISTICS WHICH MIGHT INHIBIT DATA

Loose Coupling

This term refers to the degree to which the various units of any organization are coordinated with and dependent upon one another. For example, how likely is it that a decision made by top management will be implemented at the lower operational levels? Is the coordination among levels tight or loose? Typically within school districts, the administrative arrangements linking board members and the central administrator with classroom instructional activities are very loose. District-level policy decisions relating to instruction may not be routinely implemented in the classroom (Goodlad and Klein, 1970; Meyer, 1977). The policy makers' intent may be misunderstood, changed, or ignored by classroom teachers. Thus, for example, district administrators who want to increase teachers' routine and systematic use of testing results within their own classrooms may have to take unusual and nonordinary steps to effect such behavior changes.

Teacher Isolation

Another reason why district policy-level decisions related to instruction may not be carried out in the classroom is because teachers often work behind closed doors isolated from one another and from external supervision. Consequently, it is difficult for supervisors to influence the teachers' daily activities (Lortie, 1975). Districts that intend to use evaluation and testing data to influence teacher decision-making will likely have to search for and institutionalize ways to overcome teacher isolation.

Permeable Boundaries

School districts' organizational boundaries can and often are breached by external agencies—witness external regulations or mandates from the courts or the state and federal governments. Local interest groups can often put pressure on school-district decision makers. Societal influences such as population shifts, increases in immigration, inflation, and changing tax structures also affect districts. School districts therefore have to continually adjust their activities so as to meet changing and sometimes conflicting demands and priorities (Pfeffer and Salancik, 1978). Given this boundary premeability, it is likely that school districts will have to give attention to federal, state, and local community interests in and demands for specific types of testing and evaluation data.

Goal Ambiguity

In our pluralistic society undergoing rapid social change, the stated goals of schooling seem to shift rapidly. Not only do the goals change; they are often expressed in ambiguous terms. Unlike organizations in the private sector with a profitability "bottom line," public schools must struggle with the difficulties of measuring their successes in "developing responsible citizens," creating "safe drivers," or "impressing students with an appreciation of their historical heritage." The students' attainment of these goals is often difficult to chart. In summary, there is considerable disagreement in our society about the priorities and standards for students' educational achievements. Factors such as these often diminish the utility of test data as credible measures of a school district's success in educating children. However, in districts where, for example, a community consensus might have been reached on goals such as achievement in basic skills, testing data has higher credibility.

In view of these generic school district organizational characteristics, it seemed unlikely to us that most districts would naturally and easily integrate testing and evaluation data with instructional decision-making. It did seem plausible that, in some districts, a combination of external environmental factors combined with the interests and skills of particular individuals within the districts might lead to strong administrative linkages among testing, evaluation, and instruction.

RESEARCH STRATEGY

Our project began by looking about for a small number of districts that had a reputation for linking evaluation or testing with instruction. Using previous CSE research and extensive telephone interviews with colleagues in school districts, state departments of education, other universities, and research institutions, we identified 40 districts that were thought to have linked their testing and evaluation activities with instructional decision-making in some manner. From these nominees, a final sample of six districts was selected. While these districts cannot be viewed as representative of all school districts, they do exhibit characteristics that represent the diversity of American school districts, such as differences in size (large/small), student demographics (affluent/below-average income, racially homogeneous/racially heterogeneous), and locale (urban/suburban).

For the past year, we have conducted fieldwork in four of these districts in order to describe the management structures by which test and evaluation data about students are translated into information that has instructional consequences. We analyzed documents and conducted over 40 interviews in each district built around three questions:

(1) *What?* What kind of linking system do these districts have and how does it work? How mature or fully developed is the linkage between testing, evaluation, and instruction?

(2) *So what?* Has there been any payoff from these linking efforts? Presumably the district linkage system was developed to accomplish some purpose; what evidence is there that the linking system has had its intended effect?

(3) *Why?* If most districts are not trying to link testing and evaluation with instructional decision-making, why are these districts the exception? In what environment do they operate? What was the history of their efforts? Were they planned? Who were the critical actors? What were the critical events?

At present, we have completed the first year's work in four districts and are sifting through the data in an attempt to identify common properties and consistent patterns. Before sharing our preliminary observations on the four districts, we would like to provide a word picture of what the Shelter Grove district is doing to link testing data with instructional decision-making.

One Example: Shelter Grove

"What." In the Shelter Grove School District, we see a high degree of linkage—in conceptualization and in organizational mechanisms—for the purpose of individualizing instruction in the basic skills. Teaching is closely coordinated with the following: a criterion-referenced testing (CRT) system in reading and math; a district continuum in basic skills; school-site text and film resources; school-site media and learning specialists. These instructional functions and individuals are supported by a Professional Development Program which provides training in diagnostic and prescriptive teaching for principals, teacher, aides, and substitutes; by definition of the role, the principal, as the evaluator and facilitator of instruction, must be in classrooms 40 percent of the time. Furthermore, this instructional management orientation is reflected in the recruitment, selection, and promotion procedures for the staff, as well as some principal discretion in local-site budgets.

Interviews with board members, central office personnel, principals, learning specialists, and teachers revealed remarkably homogeneous perceptions about instructional purposes. The president of the school board said, "Almost everyone believes in and works hard at teaching individual kids. The kid is the most important thing. We try not to have any throwaways." A teacher said, echoing the sentiments of a dozen of her colleagues, "This District expects a lot from its teachers; it's a great place for kids; they really learn. I moved here so I could send my own kids to the schools in this District." The Coordinator of Materials said, "We really concentrate on having the children learn—basic skills first, as well as the other important things. The parents would not have it any other way."

The conceptual connection between testing and instruction is expressed differently by different people in the district. The superintendent has a management orientation toward instruction. He advocates teaching-testing-reteaching. "Testing and instruction are intimately related." The assistant superintendent is curriculum oriented. She sees testing as the "curriculum in operation." She emphasizes staff development activities for teachers in those curricular areas where student deficiencies indicate that teachers should use different teaching strategies or devote more instructional time to specific subjects. The principals in Shelter Grove see their roles as instructional leaders and understand that they are required by the district to spend time in each classroom. They are familiar with the daily instructional program, as well as with the progress of individual children within their relatively small schools. They use the test scores of students to discuss school-level plans, grade-level plans, and classroom-level plans with teachers.

"So What?" In Shelter Grove, the teaching-testing-training cycle seems to be part of teachers' daily lives in the classroom. They were aware of all the operations which were intended by the district to support their individualization of instruction.

All the teachers interviewed knew about the district continuum and the CRT system. They explained the roles of the learning specialist, the media specialist, the principal, and the Professional Development Program in terms that were consistent with central office administrator's intention.

For most teachers, the continuum and the related CRT directed their selection of what content to teach in the basic skills. This was more true for reading and language arts than math, where the textbook sequence was often followed. Sample quotations: "The continuum is a real working tool." "I feel comfortable about using it [the continuum]." "My teaching is aimed at it." "I use CRTs in planning. I make a list of areas to work in." "I teach to the test and that's OK." For many, it provides a well thought-out way to organize their teaching. Others like the emphasis on skills. "We teach skills here in this district. How you do it is your business."

One or two of the teachers we interviewed reacted against the centralized control of the continuum and the CRT sytsem. A teacher said, in relation to math, "I don't let the test influence what I do. I think the continuum has introduced too much in the early grades." A new teacher said, "The first year I just waded through."

For most teachers, the CRT scores are useful in grouping children and in diagnosing their progress in learning. "The CRTs don't provide too many surprises." "If I've taught it well, kids pass." The teachers welcome the diagnostic screening given to new students by the learning specialist. It helps place them in groups soon after the start of school. Teachers report that student instructional groups change frequently based on CRT results. Often they change within classrooms; sometimes between classes. The learning specialist facilitates this process by conferring with teachers after each CRT administration. The media specialists advise the learning specialists and the teachers on specific student-appropriate material.

The Professional Development Program got high marks from teachers. They reported that the level-one and level-two courses (in objectives and in diagnostic/prescriptive teaching) are not duplicates of what they had in preservice courses. "PDP makes me aware of what I do. I never got this in college."

"*Why?*" Shelter Grove is a small elementary school district, consisting of seven elementary schools in which there are 132 teachers, seven learning specialists, seven principals, and 3000 children.

Shelter Grove seems an ideal community in which to try an educational experiment leading to improved educational excellence for children. The community and the school district have not been beset by many of the social problems plaguing other areas in the country. There has been no major increase or decrease in population. There exists no large group of children with English-language difficulties. There exist no major political or economic divisions within the community. The community of Shelter Grove is relatively homogeneous. Only 10 percent of the children going to Shelter Grove schools are minority.

The adults in Shelter Grove are mostly professionals or work in technical occupations. Shelter Grove is a bedroom community serving a variety of urban centers located within 50 miles of the community. The community has been stable with very few people moving out. The population has been gradually increasing, due to new housing in the area.

The district is likewise stable, with 55 percent of teachers in the district more than 10 years, and 46 percent of principals long-termers. There is a small central office consisting of 5 professionals and 15 support staff. Of these individuals, 80 percent have been with the District more than ten years.

Within the District, there seems to be general consensus that learning is important and that children are important. Although this is the rhetoric of most school districts, professionals in Shelter Grove seem to be willing to act in light of this concern, even when such actions require more work, some reorientation in their thinking, and some readjustment of territories.

Preliminary Observation on Our Four School Districts

Environmental context. It is self-evident that school districts exist in a social and historical context, as well as within a particular community. It is also self-evident, but sometimes overlooked, that the individuals working within school districts and classrooms are participants in the social and cultural ambience of their times. Additionally they are members of their professional educational communities, simultaneously shaping them and being shaped by them. What struck us forcibly about our example and the other three districts in which we worked was the influence that various environments had upon the district personnel's thinking and actions.

For example, we were told repeatedly that the parent population in the four districts were concerned about their children's ability to read, write, and do arithmetic. This emphasis on basic skills was translated by each district in accordance with the professional orientation of its administrators. In Shelter Grove, the diagnostic/prescriptive approach reflected the prevailing instructional orientation of the two universities from which the principal staff members had received their degrees. In another district where their professional training had not been so recent, district administrators responded to the community's wishes by going district-wide with fundamental schools after only a brief year-long voluntary program.

One of the striking similarities we noticed among three of our four districts was the large amount of turmoil within which each operated. One district was preoccupied with responding to court desegragation directives which necessitated district-wide management changes and changes in the autonomy teachers in minority-isolated schools will have in instructional decision-making. The district that was moving quickly to transform all of its elementary schools into fundamental schools was under pressure from a conservative school board representing a community becoming more "white collar" in composition. A third district was struggling with a sudden increase in minority and non-English-speaking students who added to an already diverse mix of students. The district was investing enormous time and energy in managing effective instruction for minority children with limited English-speaking capability.

All these district officials were daily inventing solutions to deal with these immediate problems; they felt no certainty that solutions or procedures they invented for this year's problems would be appropriate for dealing with next year's problems.

In the fourth district—the example cited above—these particular societal tensions were not present. However, during the period of our research, a heated unification election was held. The outcome was causing the district to shift from an elementary school district to a unified K-12 district.

In each of our four districts, then, there was evidence of what might be termed goal diffuseness and boundary permeability. The external environment had frequently invaded the districts' boundaries—court mandates, demands for bilingual programs, population changes, unification elections—and forced district administrators to somewhat redirect their energies. Under these circumstances, many district goals had been modified. District officials had difficulty in maintaining long-term consistency in ordering their priorities and pursuing their goals (March and Olsen, 1976). Given these external conditions, district abilities to develop and implement long-term plans had been severely challenged.

In view of these factors, we felt that it would be surprising if testing of children for the purpose of evaluating and improving instruction was uppermost in the minds of school officials. In the four districts we studied, however, testing and evaluation activities and their linkages to instructional improvement were receiving district-wide attention, although admittedly, it was not the first concern of district officials. Paradoxically, in all four districts the impetus for use of testing and evaluation data seemed to come from the same pressures in the environment which made planning difficult. For example, in the district moving toward fundamental schools, test scores were being considered by the board both as evidence of the effectiveness of the revised program and as a monitoring device for teachers' use in tracking student progress. Shelter Grove's comprehensive criterion-referenced testing (CRT) system had been developed in response to community and administrative interests in individualizing instruction for students. In our heterogeneous district, state assessment tests were being analyzed to see how the curriculum for various populations matched the specifications of the items. It seems that local environmental forces interacted with state and federal requirements to influence district officials to take actions linking testing and evaluation with instruction.

Personnel. One notable characteristic evident in our four districts was the professional interest key personnel had in instructional improvement. A second characteristic was the stability of staff. In spite of changes at the superintendent level, the individuals responsible for curriculum, instruction, and supervision of elementary and secondary levels had, in each district, worked together over a long period of time. In all four districts, these individuals had evolved methods of communicating with one another and resolving difficulties. This stability, rather than leading to stagnation, seems to have contributed in three of the four districts to a sense of direction more coherent than one would have thought possible given the other organizational and environmental instabilities.

A testing/evaluation/instructional subsystem. Although the four districts differed from one another in their size, organization, and structure, they each had developed—some more completely than others—a testing, evaluation, and instruction (T/E/I) linking subsystem. Such a subsystem was not a formal structure that appeared on the school district organizational chart; instead, it was an alignment of individuals or departments that had, for a variety of reasons, made informal and formal arrangement that enhanced linkage. The subsystem, in some cases, consisted of two people, in others more, depending on the size of the district and the way in which the subsystem was defined. It was not limited to those individuals necessarily concerned with testing and evaluation.

ELEMENTS NECESSARY FOR LINKING EVALUATION AND TESTING DATA WITH INSTRUCTION

Three components seemed to be necessary in order for the aforementioned subsystem to function: ideas, operations, and coordinating mechanisms.

By *ideas,* we mean those beliefs, goals, and assumptions—sometimes acknowledged, sometimes not—that guide the district's activities. In our four districts, both implicit and explicit ideas informed the districts' subsystems. In those districts where ideas about testing, evaluation, instruction, and management were realistic, accurate, and complete, the subsystem evolved and operated successfully. Where ideas were faulty, incompatible with one another, or not fully shared by managers, the subsystem seemed to falter. In Shelter Grove, the guiding ideas shared by most administrators and teachers were that diagnostic/prescriptive teaching and testing were needed to ensure individualized instruction. By contrast, in the district moving toward fundamental schools, ideas about how and why to use test data for instructional planning were fragmented, imperfectly understood, or disputed by many people.

By *operations* we mean those individuals, organizational arrangements, and technical capacities that enable the district to implement and sustain the district's ideas. Districts must have high quality personnel and the full range of operations in order to manage a T/E/I linking subsystem. In Shelter Grove, the district wanted to provide test results to teachers quickly so as to increase their practical value. They therefore needed computer programming skills and access to appropriate computer facilities to insure that turnaround time would not constitute a problem. Likewise, when this district wished teachers to take prescriptive action in relation to diagnostic testing and it was found that the teachers were not skilled in how to do this, the district provided them with appropriate in-service training. In this district, both computer operations and staff development were considered essential operations for linking testing and evaluation with instruction.

By *coordinating mechanisms* we mean both formal and informal structures and networks that increase communication of ideas, decisions, and actions. As we have noted earlier, school districts have often been characterized as loosely coupled; that is, communication and coordination among the various subunits are often irregular or incomplete. In many districts, the curriculum division and school principals and the testing and evaluation unit are often surprisingly uninformed about each others' activities and problems. For a T/E/I linking subsystem to work, it seems necessary that the various operations and individuals who manage them be brought together for communication and/or decision-making purposes. In our small district, as an example, this was accomplished through somewhat informal means as well as by weekly meetings of various staffs. In our other districts, coordinating mechanisms took the form of reporting relationships, memo writing, and so on.

SUMMARY

We have presented some preliminary thoughts about the conditions which discourage school districts from linking externally-mandated testing or evaluation activities with instructional decision-making; we have also indicated that some few school districts have indeed developed the ideas, operations, and coordinating mechanisms which permit the linking of testing or evaluation with instruction. During our second and third years we will describe more completely those environmental and management factors which impede and those which contribute to successful district utilization of data from tests and evaluations for locally initiated instructional improvement.

Underlying our work are the two basic points we have tried to emphasize in this chapter:

(1) The evaluation and testing communities must more diligently attend to the characteristics of administrators and teachers working within the district environment, if they expect testing and evaluation efforts to be used at the local level to improve instruction.

(2) The linking of testing and evaluation with instruction does not happen within districts, schools, and classrooms without management, intention, and effort. District-wide subsystems, informed by certain ideas and containing a range of related operations and a variety of coordinating mechanisms, seemed to be needed. The search for answers as to why such subsystems evolve, how they can operate effectively, and how they can be facilitated is worthy of continued attention and support.

REFERENCES

ALKIN, M. C., R. DAILLAK, and P. WHITE (1979) Using Evaluation: Does Evaluation Make a Difference? Beverly Hills: Sage.

CALLAHAN, R. C. (1962) Education and the Cult of Efficiency. Chicago: University of Chicago Press.

DAILLAK, R. H.. (1980) Evaluators at Work. Los Angeles: Center for the Study of Evaluation, UCLA Graduate School of Education.

DAVID, J. (1978) Local Uses of Title I Evaluation. Palo Alto, CA: Stanford Educational Policy Research Center.

GOODLAD, J. and M. F. KLEIN (1970) Behind the Classroom Door. Belmont, CA: Wadsworth.

HOLLEY, F. (1980) "Evaluation utilization: is it easier to move a mountain than a molehill?" Presented at the annual meeting of the American Educational Research Association, Boston, April.

LYON, C. D., L. DOSCHER, P. McGRANAHAN and R. C. WILLIAMS (1978) Evaluation and School Districts. Los Angeles: Center for the Study of Evaluation, UCLA Graduate School of Education.

MARCH, J. G. and J. P. OLSEN (1976) Ambiguity and Choice in Organizations. Bergen, Norway: Universitets forlaget.

MEYER, J. W. (1977) "Research on school district organizations." Presented at the annual Sociology of Education Association conference, San Diego.

PATTON, M. Q. (1978) Utilization-Focused Evaluation. Beverly Hills: Sage.

PFEFFER, J. and G. SALANCIK (1978) The External Control of Organizations: A Resource Dependence Perspective. New York: Harper & Row.

WEISS, C. H. [ed.] (1972) Evaluating Action Programs. Boston: Allyn & Bacon.

ABOUT THE AUTHORS

Carol B. Aslanian is Director of the Office of Adult Learning Services at the College Board in New York City. In this capacity, she is responsible for the design and development of new programs to improve the services of colleges and universities to adult learners. She recently completed a national study on the causes and timing of adult learning and co-authored its report, *Americans in Transition: Life Changes As Reasons For Adult Learning.* Her earlier work focused on the evaluation of educational programs at the local, state, and national levels. This included measuring the effectiveness of education and work programs, improving field test procedures to assess new curricula, and identifying ways to increase the utility of evaluation data for policy decisions. Ms. Aslanian has a B.S. from Cornell University and an M.Ed. from Harvard University. She is co-chair of the Communications Committee of the Evaluation Research Society and co-editor of the 1981 Sage Research Progress Series in Evaluation, of which this volume is one of three.

Adrianne Bank is Associate Director of the Center for the Study of Evaluation at UCLA where she co-directs a project dealing with testing, evaluation, and instruction in school districts. She is the author of two books: *A Practical Guide to Program Planning,* and *Guidebook for Evaluating Dissemination Activities.* She has done research and provided evaluation services to, among others, the National Diffusion Network, UNESCO, the American Bar Association and the Los Angeles Unified School District.

Robert F. Boruch, Professor of Psychology and Education at Northwestern University, directs the Methodology and Evaluation Research Division. He holds appointments with the Centers for Probability and Statistics and for Urban Affairs and Public Policy. He is the author and editor of a number of books on applied research including *Assuring Confidentiality of Data in Social Research* (University of Pennsylvania, 1979), *Reanalyzing Program Evaluations* (Jossey-Bass, 1981), and *Social Experimentation* (Academic, 1974). Boruch serves on a number of research committees of the National Academy of Sciences, the Social Science Research Council, and is a frequent consultant to research agencies in the United States and abroad.

Jerome Johnston is an Associate Research Scientist at the University of Michigan's Institute for Social Research. He received his Ph.D. from the University of Michigan in was a visiting professor in the Educational Psychology department at the University of Nebraska—Lincoln where she taught graduate level statistics, measurement, and data Education and Psychology. During the last 15 years he has directed a number of national studies on education and youth, including portions of the Youth in Transition Project, evaluations of the Youth Conservation Corps, and several studies of the effects of prosocial television programming on children. In his work he has tried to marry an interest in how children learn with a concern for developing research designs which will enhance the utilization of results by lay audiences.

Mary M. Kennedy is a Senior Research Associate at the Huron Institute in Cambridge, Massachusetts. The chapter she has contributed to this volume derives from a series of case studies of how local school districts have used evaluation and test information. Prior to joining the Institute she has spent six years in the U.S. Office of Education where she first worked on the national evaluation of the Follow Through Program's planned variation study, and later designed and implemented the national evaluation of the Education for All Handicapped Children Act (P.L. 94-142).

Doren L. Madey, currently on leave from NTS Research Corporation, is a consultant for The Rand Corporation where she is examining the effects of federal laws on local operations. A research analyst at NTS since 1975, she directed the NIE-funded study of the State Capacity Building Program. Her research interests and publications focus on bridging the gap between research and practice and implementing public policy.

Donna M. Mertens is a Research Specialist in the Evaluation and Policy Division of the National Center for Research in Vocational Education at Ohio State University in Columbus. She was formerly the Coordinator of Evaluation for the Appalachian Community Service Network, a telecommunications-based continuing education program. She obtained her Ph.D. from the Department of Educational Psychology and Counseling at the University of Kentucky in 1977, where she specialized in evaluation and research design and statistical analysis.

Dr. Carl D. Novak is currently senior Evaluator for Educational Service Unit 18 (ESU 18) where he heads the Evaluation Team and is a Senior Research Scientist with the American Institutes for Research. Prior to joining ESU 18, Dr. Novak was an evaluator for the Lincoln (NE) Public Schools. He has also been associated with the Nebraska State Department of Education, first as State Title I Evaluator and then as an Administrative Consultant in the Planning, Evaluation and Management Section.

A. Jackson Stenner has been President and Director of NTS Research Corporation since 1974. He has acted as principal investigator for a number of educational evaluations at the national, state, and local level, and directed a national norming of four affective instruments. Research interests and publications for the past several years have focused on multibehavioral effects of poverty and methodological innovations in multivariate data analysis and measurement theory.

Dr. Pat A. Thompson is an Associate Research Scientist with the American Institutes for Research (AIR) where she primarily works as part of the Technical Assistance Center (TAC) staff servicing Region VII. In this capacity Dr. Thompson manages the offsite TAC office located in Lincoln, Nebraska. Prior to joining AIR, Dr. Thompson analysis courses, and was co-director of the Nebraska Evaluation and Research Center.

Richard C. Williams is an Associate Professor and Chairman of the Specialization in Administrative and Policy Studies in the UCLA Graduate School of Education. He is also a faculty associate with UCLA's Center for the Study of Evaluation, where he co-directs a project dealing with testing, evaluation, and instruction in school districts. His research and publications have focused on educational innovation and change, administrative theory, collective bargaining and evaluation utilization. He has been a consultant to the research division of I/D/E/A, the Rand Corporation, and the Organization for Economic Cooperation and Development.